Growing Up in
India

Other titles in the *Growing Up Around the World* series include:

Growing Up in Brazil

Growing Up in Canada

Growing Up in China

Growing Up in Germany

Growing Up in Iran

Growing Up in Italy

Growing Up in Japan

Growing Up in Mexico

Growing Up in Russia

Growing Up in
India

Andrea C. Nakaya

San Diego, CA

© 2018 ReferencePoint Press, Inc.
Printed in the United States

For more information, contact:
ReferencePoint Press, Inc.
PO Box 27779
San Diego, CA 92198
www.ReferencePointPress.com

LIBRARY OF CONGRESS CATALOGING-IN-PUBLICATION DATA

Names: Nakaya, Andrea C., 1976– author.
Title: Growing Up in India/by Andrea C. Nakaya.
Description: San Diego, CA: ReferencePoint Press, [2017] | Audience: Grade 9
    to 12. | Includes bibliographical references and index.
Identifiers: LCCN 2017010630 (print) | LCCN 2017030517 (ebook) | ISBN
    9781682822142 (eBook) | ISBN 9781682822135 (hardback)
Subjects: LCSH: Families—India—Juvenile literature. |
    Children—India—Social conditions—Juvenile literature. | India—Social
    life and customs—Juvenile literature.
Classification: LCC HQ670 (ebook) | LCC HQ670 .N35 2017 (print) | DDC
    306.850954--dc23
LC record available at https://lccn.loc.gov/2017010630

CONTENTS

India at a Glance	**6**
Chapter One India and Its People	**8**
Chapter Two Home and Family	**20**
Chapter Three Education and Work	**33**
Chapter Four Social Life	**44**
Chapter Five Religion	**55**
Source Notes	**67**
For Further Research	**73**
Index	**75**
Picture Credits	**79**
About the Author	**80**

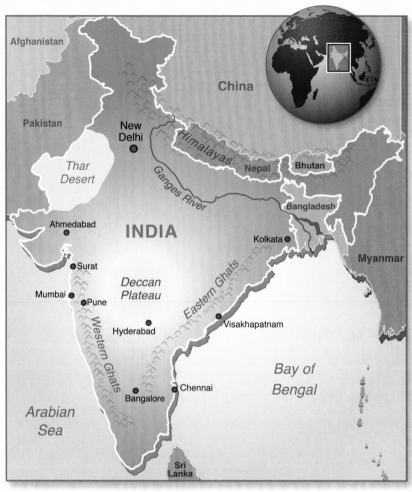

Afghanistan

China

Pakistan

New Delhi

Himalayas

Nepal

Bhutan

Thar Desert

Ganges River

Bangladesh

Ahmedabad

INDIA

Kolkata

Myanmar

Surat

Mumbai

Pune

Deccan Plateau

Eastern Ghats

Hyderabad

Visakhapatnam

Western Ghats

Bay of Bengal

Bangalore

Chennai

Arabian Sea

Sri Lanka

Official Name
Republic of India

Size
1,269,219 square miles
(3,287,263 sq. km)

Total Population ●
1,266,883,598

Youth Population
0–14 years: 27.71%
15–24 years: 17.99%

Ethnic Groups
Indo-Aryan: 72%; Dravidian: 25%;
Mongoloid and other: 3%

Religions ●
Hindu: 79.8%; Muslim: 14.2%;
Christian: 2.3%; Sikh: 1.7%

Capital
New Delhi

Type of Government
Federal parliamentary republic

Most Common Languages
Hindi: 41%; Bengali: 8.1%;
Telugu: 7.2%

Currency ●
Indian rupee

Industries
Textiles, chemicals, food processing,
steel, transportation equipment,
cement, mining, petroleum, machinery,
software, pharmaceuticals

Internet Users ●
325.4 million (26% of the population)

Literacy
71% of the population over age 15
(81.3% of males, 60.6% of females)

CHAPTER ONE

India and Its People

According to a 2014 report by the United Nations Population Fund, India has the largest number of young people between the ages of ten and twenty-four of any country in the world. These 356 million young people live a multitude of different lifestyles. Some live in one-room huts in small villages, while others live in mansions in huge cities; some are Hindu, while others are Muslim; and some go to school, while others spend their days working in factories. One of the things that characterizes India is its diversity. It is a very large country, containing more than 1 billion people, and these people live in all kinds of ways.

Geography

India is located on the continent of Asia and shares borders with Pakistan, China, Nepal, Bhutan, Myanmar, and Bangladesh. India is also bordered by water: the Arabian Sea, the Bay of Bengal, and the larger Indian Ocean. Overall, the country of India is so large that there is considerable variation in geography and climate. In some areas the weather and landscape are harsh, and people must work hard just to survive. For example, the Himalayas, or Himalaya Mountains, stretch along part of India's northern border. They contain the tallest mountain peaks in the world, and weather extremes and rugged terrain make life there challenging. Jane Dyson has spent time in the village of Bemni in this region. She talks about how hard the families there must work to grow food to feed themselves and their animals. Because the land is so mountainous, farming involves a lot of hard physical labor. She says, "Fields are hacked out of the mountainside, prepared by cattle pulling wooden ploughs, and harvested with sickles and blistered hands. All the crops—wheat, barley, pulses, hay for the livestock—must be hauled up the mountain to be stored."[1] She stresses that everyone in the village, even young people, must work together at these tasks to ensure the survival of the village. However, despite the hard work, Dyson observes that the young people in Bemni also make time for play. She says, "Amid the gruelling labour, the children also had lots of fun. They made impromptu picnics and fooled around in the forest. . . . They'd bombard me with snowballs, or make up playful rhymes about me."[2]

Daily life is also challenging in India's Thar Desert, located in the northwestern part of the country. Temperatures in this region can reach 120°F (49°C) in the summer, and because of the extreme heat, young people in the Thar typically live in homes made of mud bricks, with grass roofs and small windows, all of which help keep the home cool inside. Water is scarce in much of the Thar Desert, so many young people must spend a lot of time and energy collecting it. The International Development Exchange, an organization that works to alleviate poverty around the world, says, "Women walk for hours each day to collect enough water for the family. This is often the role of girls who are prevented from attending school."[3] Many people rely on seasonal ponds and streams for water, and some people in the Thar even forgo permanent homes in favor of a nomadic lifestyle so that they can go where the water is.

> "[In the Thar Desert] women walk for hours each day to collect enough water for the family. This is often the role of girls who are prevented from attending school."[3]
>
> —International Development Exchange, an organization that works to alleviate poverty around the world

Not all of India's climate is so difficult to live in, though. The country also contains large areas of lush forest and fertile farmland. One of the biggest areas of fertile land is located south of the Himalayas, in the Indo-Gangetic Plain. The area receives a large amount of rain, and the Ganges River—the longest in India—and other smaller rivers flow through it, producing rich farmland. The Ganges also supports a large number of fishers. Boys who live near the river often learn to fish with their fathers. In their free time both boys and girls enjoy swimming

Young people in West Bengal cross the Ganges River in a wooden boat—a fast and inexpensive way to travel. The longest river in India, the Ganges supports the fishing industry and provides water for the surrounding farmland.

in the river. The Indo-Gangetic Plain is India's most populous area, with many urban areas and some of India's biggest cities, including its capital, New Delhi. Another vast fertile region is located in the south of India and is called the Deccan Plateau. The plateau contains both forests and farmland and supports a wide variety of plant and animal species.

Extreme Heat

Although there are variations across the country, much of India gets very hot in the summer. The National Oceanic and Atmospheric Administration states, "India is a place that knows heat. During May—the last month before the monsoon rains arrive to cool things down—temperatures can soar to 104°F (40°C) on average. Yes, this means that a day when high temperatures in say, the northern city of New Delhi, rise to only 102°F (39°C) would mean that temperatures were below average."[4] Sometimes the country experiences heat waves, and temperatures get even hotter. For example, during a 2015 heat wave that affected much of

India, temperatures rose as high as 117°F (47°C) in some places. It was so hot that roads in New Delhi started melting.

Though most people who live in India become accustomed to the heat, the heat waves can be difficult to bear. During such times, youths flock to rivers and lakes to cool down. At night many sleep outside with their families, where it is cooler than indoors. Some families sleep on the roofs of their houses. Professional photographer Yasmin Mund visited the city of Varanasi in northern India one summer and was surprised to see just how many people were sleeping on the roofs of their homes. She says that she climbed to the roof terrace of her guesthouse to watch the sunrise. She recalls, "As I looked over the side of the balcony my mouth dropped in disbelief. Below were mothers, fathers, children, monkeys and cows sleeping soundly on the roofs of their houses."[5]

> "During May—the last month before the monsoon rains arrive to cool things down— temperatures can soar to 104°F (40°C) on average."[4]
>
> —National Oceanic and Atmospheric Administration, a US government agency that gathers data about the skies and the oceans

Monsoon Season

In addition to the heat, another defining feature of India's weather is the yearly monsoon. Monsoons are heavy rains that typically occur throughout much of the country from June to September. These rains are both beneficial and problematic. They are beneficial because they provide relief from the summer heat and much-needed water for irrigation. Therefore, most people in India welcome their arrival, and it is common to see young people—indeed, people of all ages—joyously frolicking in the rain when the monsoon arrives. Writer Amrit Dhillon says:

Monsoon for Indians is sweet and exhilarating because it signals the end of torrid, diabolical heat, often of 100F or more. So, when the skies turn grey and clouds appear, the excitement mounts. People start smiling. Spirits soar. . . . In minutes, the earth is swirling with so much water you feel fish might leap forth. Children dance in the streets. Strangers smile at one another in delight. The aroma released by rain on sun-baked earth is intoxicating.[6]

Residents of Kolkata wade through a flooded street after heavy rains. India's yearly monsoon season brings much-needed water but also causes severe flooding in cities.

However, so much rain falls during monsoon season that it can cause major flooding, ruining homes and disabling transportation systems. The flooding also spreads disease, as drains overflow and water runs through the streets. Steve Richards, who works at the children's charity World Vision, shares what some Indian young people from a slum in the city of Patna have to say about the monsoons. One comments, "In the monsoon my house leaks. In monsoons we put plastics over our roof. Outside water gathers. Once water gathers we have to make the drains and then the drains get full."[7] Another describes the pollution that the rain causes, saying, "From the muddy roads, very bad smells comes out. When we take bath in that rain we fall sick. We have to eat medicine, it is very bad taste."[8]

Population

Every day, India's large population grows even larger. The country already has more than 1.2 billion people, which is the second-largest population in the world after China. In a 2015 report, the United Nations predicts that India's population will surpass that of China within seven years. In addition, it forecasts that the population will continue to grow after that, reaching 1.7 billion by 2050. Young people constitute a significant percentage of India's large and rapidly growing population. According to the country's most recent census information—from 2011—41 percent of the population is under age eighteen. Overall, experts predict that India will be the youngest country in the world by 2020.

India's huge population is also one of the most ethnically diverse in the world. According to the *CIA World Factbook*, 72 percent of the population is Indo-Aryan, and 25 percent is Dravidian. However, within these two main groups is great ethnic diversity, with thousands of different ethnicities in total. India is also home to a multitude of languages. The country's constitution recognizes twenty-two official languages; of these, Hindi is the most widely spoken. In addition, according to the country's most recent census, there are one hundred other languages that are each spoken by at least ten thousand people. Yet even this number is far from the final total. Researchers also report that there are hundreds more languages spoken throughout the country by smaller numbers of people. For example, in 2013 the People's Linguistic Survey of India reported on a comprehensive survey conducted over four years, stating that it found 780 languages overall.

Poverty and Lack of Sanitation

The majority of India's population—about three-quarters—live in rural areas. The rest live in its crowded cities. No matter where they live though, many people are affected by poverty, which is a major feature of life in the country. A 2015 CNN report summarizes some of the findings of India's Socioeconomic and Caste Census, which was conducted in 2011, and reveals details about the poverty in which many Indians live. The report says, "Of the 300 million households surveyed, an overwhelming majority (73%) live in villages. Of this rural population, less than 5% earn enough to pay taxes, only 2.5% own a 4-wheeler vehicle and less than 10%

have salaried jobs." Overall, the CNN report concludes, "the bulk of the Indian population is still overwhelmingly poor."[9]

Some people are so poor that they are classified as living below the poverty line, meaning that they do not have enough money to obtain basic food, clothing, and shelter. By the most recent estimate of the *CIA World Factbook*, almost 30 percent of India's population falls into this classification. Extreme poverty is driving many people out of India's rural villages into the cities, where they hope to find better economic opportunities. As a result, India's rural/urban mix is changing, and every year a greater percentage of its population lives in the cities. However, moving to the city often does not lift people out of poverty; poverty rates are extremely high there too.

In addition to poverty, another major problem affecting many people is a widespread lack of basic sanitation services. Cities and towns in most developed countries have facilities to collect and process trash and sewage to prevent pollution and disease; however, this is not the case in most of India. Many Indians do not have access to toilets or clean water, and it is common to see trash and human waste littering the sides of the streets. According to a 2016 report by WaterAid, a safe water and sanitation advocacy organization, about 18 percent of urban homes in India do not have toilets. Some of the people who live in these homes use public toilets, but many must go to the bathroom outside. Even the toilets that do exist do not necessarily solve the problem, because according to a 2013 report in the *Times of India*, almost 80 percent of India's sewage is not treated and flows into water sources such as rivers and lakes. As a result, many of India's bodies of water, including the groundwater that people drink, is contaminated by sewage.

India's Roads

Another distinctive feature of life in India is its roads, which are often busy and chaotic due to the vast number of people using them. When they turn sixteen, Indian youths are old enough to drive on these roads. They can apply for a learner's driver's license by taking a written exam, and if they pass, they are permitted to drive a moped or a gearless motorcycle. At eighteen

Collectivist Culture

While some cultures raise their young people with an emphasis on autonomy and individuality, Indian young people are taught that family and group relationships and responsibilities are far more important. Aneesh Joshi, who has lived half his life in India and half in the United States, explains India's collectivist culture by comparing it to US culture. He says, "American culture is individualist. There is more importance placed on individual goals, initiatives and achievement. On the other hand, Indian culture is collectivist. As such, the rights of families, communities, and the collective supersede those of the individual." Becky Stephen, who has led numerous cross-cultural training programs, stresses that people in India do things as a family or a group. She says, "There is no such thing as 'my property,' 'my space,' or 'my decision.'" In fact, she says that young people who act independently are seen as selfish. This collectivist view is instilled in young people in many different ways. For example, older siblings and cousins are expected to play with younger ones and look after them.

Aneesh Joshi, comment on Quora, "How Is the Lifestyle of an Indian Teen Different from Teens of Other Countries?," September 13, 2014. www.quora.com.

Becky Stephen, *Culture Smart! India*. London: Kuperard, p. 53.

they may take the driving exam that allows them to obtain a permanent license and drive a car or motorcycle with gears. Many report that it is relatively easy to obtain these licenses, and as a result it is common to see Indian young people driving on the country's roads.

Some research has shown that a large number of young people actually drive at a far younger age than sixteen. For example, according to a 2015 report in the *Times of India*, when teachers asked a ninth-grade class in Mumbai how many had driven a car or motorcycle, almost 90 percent raised their hands. In a study published in the *International Journal of Applied Research* in 2016, researchers investigating driving in the southern Indian state of Kerala found that a high percentage of youths drove, most of them with their parents' approval. Eighty-one percent said they had driven at least a few times, and almost 40 percent said they drove frequently. Writer for the *Hindu* Kritika Sharma explains some of the reasons that parents allow their underage children to drive in the city of Delhi:

> With most Delhiites possessing more than one vehicle, including cars and two wheelers, there is a huge chance of children taking up driving at a young age. Many parents do not have a problem with it, as it comes in handy for meeting routine needs and in case of an emergency. This, according to them, is a situation when someone at home is unwell and needs to be driven to the hospital or is late for their train or a flight.[10]

Whether or not they have a valid license, young people who drive in India face a challenging environment. India's roads—particularly in urban areas—are a chaotic mix of pedestrians, cars, buses, rickshaws, motorcycles, and even cows, and disregard for

Indian youths can start driving once they turn sixteen. Navigating the roads is challenging in urban areas, as streets are packed with pedestrians, cars, buses, rickshaws, motorcycles, and even cows.

road rules is common. As a result, there is a very high rate of accidents. Aastha Sharma, a public health professional from Harvard School of Public Health, explains:

> There is rampant cell-phone use while behind the wheel, drunken driving, jaywalking, disregard for seatbelts or helmets and generally poor driving ethics. This is compounded by unsafe cars, poor roads, absence of sidewalks and pedestrian crossings, faulty parking, road encroachments, non-functional traffic lights and poor road night lighting. All of these combine to make the perfect recipe for an accident.[11]

Sharma says that in India there is approximately one traffic accident every minute and one traffic-related death every four minutes. A traffic officer in Mumbai explains that it is impossible to stop all of the dangerous behavior that occurs on India's roads due to the sheer number of people using them. "We can catch a maximum of two offenders at a time—maximum," he says. "[The rest] just go. There are no consequences."[12]

> "There is rampant cell-phone use while behind the wheel, drunken driving, jaywalking, disregard for seatbelts or helmets and generally poor driving ethics."[11]
>
> —Aastha Sharma, a public health professional from the Harvard School of Public Health

Government

The government that makes and enforces India's many laws is a relatively new one. It was formed in 1947, after the country finally broke free of the British rule it had been under for almost a century. The government is democratic, with an executive, legislative, and judicial branch. The legislative branch comprises two houses, the Lok Sabha and Rajya Sabha, which make the laws, and a prime minister, who is the head of the government. India also has a president, who serves for a five-year term. Overall, the country has more than one thousand different political parties, so there is often no majority winner in an election. This means that politicians commonly form coalition governments, in which several parties cooperate to govern.

Vaccination

India is one of the largest producers of vaccines in the world. It sells these vaccines to the World Health Organization, United Nations Children's Fund, and more than one hundred different countries. However, although the country has been successful at exporting vaccines, it has been less successful at vaccinating its own people. Many young people in India die from preventable illnesses because they do not receive recommended childhood vaccinations. Experts believe that this is due in part to a lack of health care funding and to a lack of public demand for childhood vaccination—for instance, parents not knowing about the importance of vaccination or distrusting vaccination. In 2016 researchers from the University of Michigan School of Public Health reported on the vaccination of young children in India. Matthew Boulton, a senior author of the study, found that only 12 percent of children get the measles vaccine by the required age of nine months. He warns, "India's childhood vaccination rate is simply too low to successfully control transmission of disease and prevent measles-related childhood illnesses and deaths." In addition to measles, many Indian youths get sick or die from numerous other illnesses that could be prevented by vaccination. In 2014 the government took action to try to improve vaccination statistics by launching Mission Indradhanush. This initiative aims to ensure that by 2020, all children under age two are immunized against seven major life-threatening diseases. As a result of Mission Indradhanush, childhood vaccination in India has been increasing.

Quoted in Institute for Healthcare Policy & Innovation, University of Michigan, "Most Kids in India Lack Timely Vaccinations," June 2, 2016. http://ihpi.umich.edu.

Because such a large, and growing, percentage of India's population consists of young people, they have the potential to significantly affect politics. Research shows that an increasing percentage of young people are participating in the political system. For example, the Centre for the Study of Developing Societies reports that in 2011, about 70 percent of urban young people were interested in politics, compared with only 45 percent in 2009. Employment is one of the most important issues to young voters. Moreover, many young people are motivated to be active in politics because they have a desire to change what they believe to be a corrupt political system. This is the case with Raghav Chadha, a young politician who studied accounting in school, then got into politics because he wanted to wipe out government corruption. He states, "Over the past few decades, . . . [the] objective [of politicians] has been to abuse power and to make money. . . . Politics has been devoid of patriotism: it has become a bad word, a bad business; it is not considered noble or respectable."[13]

It is not just in politics that Indian young people have the potential to wield considerable power. Somini Sengupta, author of *The End of Karma: Hope and Fury Among India's Young*, explains, "India has the largest concentration of young people in the world at any time in recorded history—420 million Indians are between the ages of 15 and 34, and every month for the next several years, 1 million Indians are turning 18."[14] The beliefs and desires of such a large number of young people could strongly influence India's economy, politics, and society as a whole. In addition, because India is such a large nation and has an important impact on world affairs, the power of its young people could extend around the world. Sengupta predicts, "[The influence of India's young people is] going to shape the world for the rest of us."[15]

"India has the largest concentration of young people in the world at any time in recorded history."[14]

—Somini Sengupta, author of *The End of Karma: Hope and Fury Among India's Young*

CHAPTER TWO

Home and Family

Home and family are extremely important in India. From the moment they are born, young people are taught to value and respect their family and always stay loyal to them. N.K. Chadha, professor of psychology at the University of Delhi, and author of numerous books and articles, explains, "India . . . emphasizes family integrity, family loyalty, and family unity." He stresses, "Togetherness is what rules over here."[16] For youths in India, almost all aspects of their lives are influenced in some way by family.

Rural Life

Although family is very important to most young people, everyday life can vary considerably depending on where a young person lives and the financial status of his or her family. The majority of India's population live in villages in the countryside. Youths in these villages typically live without many of the modern conveniences that urban youths have. For example, instead of having their own bedrooms, many rural young people live with their whole family in a one-room hut made from clay, bricks, bamboo, or palm leaves. These huts usually do not have running water inside; instead, water must be fetched from the village well, a chore that young people—usually girls—help with. In some villages girls must walk miles to the well, carrying the water back in pots balanced on their heads.

In addition, many villages have only limited access to electricity. In fact, a significant number of Indian young people have never even seen an electric lightbulb. Instead, families use cow-dung patties to fuel cooking fires, or kerosene lamps for light at night. This means that most families try to cook and eat dinner before it gets dark. Children also try to finish their schoolwork before the sun sets. Journalist Tanaya Singh explains, "The alternative is the dim light of kerosene lamps, and the oil for these lamps is not affordable for the poor."[17] However, having money for kerosene lamps is not necessarily a good thing; those young people who live in homes that can afford them often suffer from health problems due to breathing in the fumes from burning kerosene.

Although a lack of electricity and other modern conveniences can make life more difficult in some ways, young people who grow up in India's countryside often report that they enjoy the re-

Women carry pitchers of water to their homes in Guwahati in northeastern India. Few people living in rural areas have access to running water and other modern conveniences.

laxed pace and neighborly atmosphere of village life. In rural India when the day's work is finished, both adults and young people typically make the most of their free time by relaxing with friends and family. Rural areas usually do not have malls, theaters, or restaurants for entertainment like the cities do, so young people typically entertain themselves by socializing with one another, or playing games such as cricket, a game played between two teams, using a leather ball and a wooden bat. When he was young, Nishad Shah spent a lot of time in the village that his mother came from. He explains, "Think of the days of your vacations in school. You probably met your friends every other day and talk for hours together. Villagers do that almost every day."[18]

> "Think of the days of your vacations in school. You probably met your friends every other day and talk for hours together. Villagers do that almost every day."[18]
>
> —Nishad Shah, a young man who lives in India

Because they spend a lot of time outside, many rural youths also feel that they have a strong connection to nature. For instance, Sandip Pawar grew up in a small village in India and laments that city life does not have the same connection. She says, "[In the city] everything is nearby but still I feel some part of my life is missing and it's my village. . . . There are all kind of facilities, hospitals, market places, malls, multiplex and big list in the cities but there is no nature touch to it. Cities only buzz but nature whispers which we can get only in villages."[19]

Living in the City

Many people choose not to live in India's villages, though—close to a third of the population live in urban areas, which are generally noisy and crowded. Many middle-class families live in small apartments; however, some young people belong to upper- or middle-class families that have enough money to escape the chaos of the cities by living in private gated communities. Life inside these communities is strikingly different from what is outside. Saritha Rai, who lives in the city of Bangalore, describes what life is like for young people who live in the Yash Enclave gated community in that city:

Inside, the streets are squeaky clean, homes have lush gardens, and there is seldom a honk heard from the cars as they cruise through, stopping to make way for kids riding bicycles, gliding by on rollerblades or chasing after cricket balls. It is a place where children also leave bicycles and skateboards outdoors without fear of theft—a situation unthinkable in any Indian city. Beyond Yash Enclave's manned gates is India's urban reality: slums, potholed and traffic choked roads, piles of garbage on street corners, traffic fumes, and a cacophonous din from the revving motors and incessant honking of the cars, buses and motorcycles.[20]

Most people are not lucky enough to enjoy such luxury, though. In fact, many young people living in India's urban areas belong to families that cannot afford even small apartments. Instead, they live in slums, where they construct homes out of scraps of wood, metal, cardboard, or anything else they can

Bathing in Public

In many parts of India, space and privacy are limited. For example, many of the country's poor are forced to bathe at public water taps or in the river, and large numbers of people live in close proximity to one another in the cities. Becky Stephen, who has traveled throughout India, gives numerous examples of these types of situations. She says, "In many rural areas, fields double as toilets. In towns, teenage boys in lungis or shorts can be found soaping up at the public water pump. In the river, women discreetly wash and change. Large numbers of people share small spaces: an extended family lives in a tiny two-room hut; a couple and their children share a bedroom in an urban apartment." As a result, India's young people learn to maintain privacy by looking away or ignoring some of the things that other people do. Stephen explains, "Indians develop the skill of looking without seeing early on."

Becky Stephen, *Culture Smart! India*. London: Kuperard, 2010, p. 86.

find. They have limited access to electricity, clean water, or even bathrooms. Journalist Jim Yardley describes the Dharavi slum in Mumbai:

> The streets smell of sewage and sweets. There are not enough toilets. There is not enough water. There is not enough space. Laborers sleep in sheds known as pongal houses, six men, maybe eight, packed into a single, tiny room—multiplied by many tiny rooms. . . . Traffic bleats. Flies and mosquitoes settle on roadside carts of fruit and atop the hides of wandering goats. Ten families share a single water tap, with water flowing through the pipes for less than three hours every day, enough time for everyone to fill a cistern or two. Toilets are communal, with a charge of 3 cents to defecate. Sewage flows through narrow, open channels, slow moving streams of green water and garbage.[21]

Young people who live in slums like this often have to bathe in public at the water tap or in the river. Some do not even have access to communal toilets and are forced to go to the bathroom

A boy sits in a slum in Mumbai. Extreme poverty and the lack of basic sanitation services are major problems in both cities and rural areas throughout the country.

outside. Mari Marcel Thekaekara lives in India and writes on human rights issues. She says that because many parts of India are so hot and humid, most Indians strive to bathe every day, so public bathing is a daily occurrence for many people. She explains, "It's difficult for the elite to even begin to understand the humiliation of a life with no privacy ever and no bathroom or toilet."[22]

> "It's difficult for the elite to even begin to understand the humiliation of a life with no privacy ever and no bathroom or toilet."[22]
>
> —Mari Marcel Thekaekara, who lives in India and writes on human rights issues

The Extended Family

While in some countries a household typically consists of a nuclear family—a couple and their children—it is common for Indians to live in an extended family instead. This means that multiple generations live in one house and share the household responsibilities. In the typical Indian extended family, children live with their parents, and when a son marries, his wife comes to live with him and his family. The extended family thus includes grandparents, aunts, uncles, and cousins. In these families the eldest males typically make the decisions, and children are expected to respect and obey their elders. Commenting in an online forum, one person who grew up in India explains, "There are strict hierarchies for how you behave with your family—it's normal for anyone from an older generation to expect your complete obedience and respect."[23]

The women in an Indian family are generally responsible for all the household chores. From a young age, girls help with these chores and gradually learn how to do all the household tasks themselves. India's National Sample Survey Organization conducted a survey from 2011 to 2012 and found that some of the chores that women and girls spend the most time on are making cow-dung patties for cooking fuel, collecting firewood, sewing and mending clothes, and collecting drinking water. It also found that in many areas, women are also responsible for fishing, husking rice, grinding grain, and preserving meat. In contrast, boys usually do not have many chores. Instead, for boys, there is usually a lot of pressure to do well in school. Another common aspect of life in an extended family is that family members share everything. Stanley Wolpert, author of a number of books about

25

India, says that in an extended household, doors rarely lock or even close. "Joint families are used to sharing, not just food, but possessions of all sorts,"[24] he says.

Young people express mixed opinions on the extended family. Some love the support and closeness such families provide. Electronics engineer Shreyas Banthalpad says that he has spent time living in both nuclear and joint (extended) families and states that he prefers the latter. He says:

> In the joint family, we were a ragged group of five cousins. We played rough (I still have the scars to prove it), had hell of a lot of fun and got into a lot of trouble too. Most of us even attended the same school! Our lives were bound to each other. Happiness, sadness, or whatever was experienced together. . . . I firmly believe the time I spent in the joint family was the best. Had a lot of fun, learnt a lot of life lessons and developed a bond with my cousins that is still very strong to this day.[25]

"Privacy? What's that? Parents have all the right to check our phones, and everything from time to time actually every time it pings or makes a noise. They have to interfere in almost everything. Space and privacy doesn't exist."[28]

—Brenda Bhaskar, an Indian teen

Apurva Gayakwad, who lives in Mumbai, agrees that a joint family provides more benefits than a nuclear one. She says, "It's an amazing feeling to come home (anytime) to many smiling and welcoming faces. Whenever you wish for it, there is almost always somebody who can give you company and/or the comfort of a listening ear. This one pro wipes out all cons :)."[26] Wolpert says that when people leave a traditional extended family home, they often find their lives lonely. However, others complain that family interferes too much in an extended household, so a growing number of urban couples are opting to live as nuclear families instead.

Parental Control

The complaint that parents are too controlling is a common one from Indian young people. Commenting in an online forum, one person who grew up in India explains that Indian young people

Child Marriage

In some parts of India, girls are married when they are very young, sometimes before they even become teenagers. Although it is illegal for girls under age eighteen to marry, in many rural areas child marriage is common and widely accepted, and law enforcement does not interfere. Some of these girls are married to boys their own age and some to older men. While some young brides are happy, child marriage can be harmful to girls because they may be forced to stop attending school, and also because young girls who become pregnant and their babies have a much higher risk of health problems than older mothers and their babies.

The United Nations Population Fund, an organization that advocates for the rights of young people, tells the stories of some child brides in India. For example, Bina Bai in the state of Madhya Pradesh was married at fourteen. The organization says, "Bina soon became pregnant. She suffered multiple health issues, and her baby died shortly after birth." It reports on another girl, Komal, who says she was forced to drop out of school and marry at sixteen. Komal says, "Sometimes, when the others are not at home, I read my old school books and hold my baby and cry."

United Nations Population Fund, "Dependent, Deprived: Child Brides in India Tell Their Stories," June 10, 2015. www.unfpa.org.

are generally expected to let their parents make many decisions about their lives, stating, "In India, it is considered normal for your parents to decide most of the things about your life. They often decide where you go to school/college, what you study, who you'll marry."[27] Indian teen Brenda Bhaskar complains that this parental control extends to the smallest aspects of her life, including her cell phone. She says, "Privacy? What's that? Parents have all the right to check our phones, and everything from time to time actually every time it pings or makes a noise. They have to interfere in almost everything. Space and privacy doesn't exist."[28]

However, although Indian parents might insist on having a lot of control over their children's lives, they typically provide for them far longer than parents in many other countries. It is common for Indian young people to live with their parents until they marry. Dipti Vaid Dedhia, Sheena Vaid Dedhia, and Nina Vaid Raoji, creators of a South Asian fashion and lifestyle blog, explain that this is based on the idea that parents take care of their children unconditionally, and in turn, the children later take care of them unconditionally. They explain:

> The parents will rarely expect any monetary contributions from the children as they believe it's their own "duty" to take care of their children. Therefore, in the Indian household, the parents will pay the mortgage and expenses needed to support their children, with the expectation that once the parents get older, they will live with their kids and be supported by them in health and finances—regardless of the living situation.[29]

The oldest son in particular is responsible for taking care of his parents when they get older. Kavya Sukumar is a young woman who grew up in India. She explains that her husband, Srini, has always known that as the oldest son in his family, he would be responsible for providing his parents with financial support. She says that his parents frequently told Srini, "Study well so you can support the family."[30]

Marriage in India

The practice of making decisions as a family unit extends to marriage. Surveys show that most marriages in India are arranged, particularly in rural areas. University professor Utpal M. Dholakia explains how an arranged marriage typically works:

> For both men and women, the individual's parents or older family members screen for and find prospective mates for further consideration through their social circle, community, or by advertising on matrimonial websites or newspapers. There is an initial meeting in a family gathering, after which the couple has a few opportunities for chaperoned courtship. At this point if neither party has vetoed the match and if they are so inclined, they may spend some time together alone.[31]

Dholakia adds that in some cases, this entire process happens in only a few days. An increasing number of people are using matchmaking websites in this process, because these sites allow them access to a larger pool of prospective mates. According to a 2015 *New York Times* report, India has more than one thousand matchmaking websites.

There are mixed opinions on the system of arranged marriage. Many young people complain that there is no consideration of their desires or feelings. Girls especially often feel that they are seen merely as a commodity. For instance, Upasana Chauhan is from the north Indian state of Haryana and says that when she was meeting families for a potential arranged marriage, the parents would sometimes inspect her as if she were a piece of property that they were considering acquiring, rather than a human being. She says, "Sometimes the mother would touch me because she wanted to check my skin and hair. Those meetings were nothing less than a terrifying flea market."[32]

A bride and groom and other family members take part in a traditional Hindu wedding ceremony. Although a growing number of young people are deciding whom they will marry, most marriages are still arranged by parents.

Others contend that the system works because families do a lot of research to help ensure that a couple will be compatible. Balaji Viswanathan, who lives in Bengaluru, explains that in non-arranged marriages, a couple often have incomplete information about one another and might make the decision to marry based primarily on physical attraction. In comparison, he says, in an arranged marriage,

> before the "date" [initial meeting] happens an enormous amount of filtering & back end work has been done to make sure things stick. . . . I was really apprehensive of arranged marriages and during my teens I swore to get married only *through love*. But, as soon as I met my future wife in an arranged setting, I knew why the process works. . . . I have observed about 30 odd marriages—in my friends & family—95% of them arranged and they have similar experiences.[33]

Despite continuing support for the system of arranged marriage, in recent years a growing number of young people—mostly in India's urban areas—have begun to take more of a role in deciding whom they will marry. Indian woman Meenakshhi Mishra explains, "Among parents, mindsets are changing. . . . Educated middle class parents are more than happy to accept their kid's choice of their partners. For example, in my family from my generation, 5 out of 9 cousins have gone for love marriages with their parents blessings. My parents were ok with love marriage concept."[34] The extent to which young people are allowed to be involved in finding a wife or husband varies. Some young people are allowed veto power over their parents' choices. Others actively search matchmaking websites with their parents to choose prospective mates whom they find attractive. In some cases young people simply meet and fall in love, and their parents agree to let them marry. However, overall, arranged marriage is still very common.

Dowry
When a couple marries, the parents of the bride will most likely be expected to give the gift of a dowry to the family of the groom. This can be money, jewelry, or other valuable items such as household

goods. The dowry tradition has existed since ancient times, and although it was forbidden by law in 1961, it remains extremely common. Kavya Sukumar says that the practice of dowry is such an integral part of life that it can significantly affect the way people live their lives. For instance, many girls are pressured into careers such as engineering in which they can earn a lot of money, because their parents believe this will make them more valuable to prospective husbands and thus decrease the amount of dowry they will have to pay. Sukumar says her sister was pressured to follow this career. She explains:

> When my sister chose to stray away from the beaten path of engineering or medicine—the only two career choices children in my extended family are given—strangers warned my parents that they would have to pay more dowry to get my sister married. My sister chose to be a fashion designer. And fashion designing, I learned then, is not very high on the list of preferred jobs in the marriage market.[35]

Some families go into debt because of a dowry. Shafeer Jan lives in the village of Nilambur in southern India. He says that dowry can be a difficult burden for a family. He recalls, "I saw how my parents struggled to save up for my sister's dowry. We all suffered as a family."[36] He reports that his parents even started skipping meals to save money for the dowry.

Unfortunately, the practice of dowry also sometimes leads to violence, in which brides are harassed or even killed by families trying to obtain a larger dowry. Donna Fernandes, the founder of the women's rights organization Vimochana, explains:

> The husband's family believes they have not received enough money for their son at the time of the wedding, perhaps because they are of a higher caste or some such reason, and that's when the harassment starts. . . . They start asking for cash, or gold, or consumer goods like washing machines or televisions. Whatever it is they believe is owed to them or was promised to them, luxury goods that they can get the bride's family to pay for.[37]

If their demands are not met, they may verbally or physically abuse the bride. In some cases brides are harassed so much that they commit suicide, or they are even murdered by the groom or his family.

Daily life in India remains strongly influenced by traditional beliefs and customs. In some cases, such as with the practice of dowry, this can result in harm such as harassment or death of brides. However, some traditions also have positive impacts, such as the focus on looking after extended family members. Home and family life in India—as in other countries all over the world—is a complicated matter that some young people embrace and others wish to change.

CHAPTER THREE

Education and Work

Education in India varies greatly, depending on where a young person lives and what type of family he or she belongs to. In many families parents believe that education is extremely important, and children in these families report that not only are they expected to attend school every day, but they are under an enormous amount of pressure to work hard and excel there. As in other countries, the goal for these young people is to use their education to find good jobs. However, some young people in India do not receive an education. There are a variety of reasons for this. Some youths belong to families that are so poor that the children must work rather than go to school. Others live in impoverished areas with a lack of teachers or schools. India's government has recognized that these problems exist, and overall the country's education system has improved significantly in recent years.

Going to School in India

Under India's 2009 Right to Education Act, school is free and compulsory for children ages six to fourteen. This schooling is called elementary school, or primary school, and consists of grades one through eight. After completing the first eight grades, children can choose to go to secondary school. Lower secondary school consists of grades nine and ten. Students then take public examinations to gain admission to upper secondary school, which consists of grades eleven and twelve. Those who want to attend a university must take public exams again in grade twelve. These exams, also called board exams, are very important because there is fierce competition to attend India's best universities. To be accepted into a good university, students must not only pass their exams but score high enough to meet that university's admission requirement.

The two most common career paths in India are medicine and engineering, since these fields are viewed as secure and high paying. Many parents strongly pressure their children to study for one of these two fields. Indian teen Brenda Bhaskar comments on this pressure, stating, "Our parents will decide whether we should go for Medical or Engineering. Because other career paths are apparently for non pointers [underachievers], right?"[38] Whether or not young people are actually interested in medicine or engineering often appears to be of little importance. For instance, eighteen-year-old Murtaza Phalisiya says that most of his friends want to study engineering or medicine so that they can earn a lot of money. "It's not really the want of knowledge that motivates them. It's a better standard of living for their families," he explains. "If you study the arts, you are scoffed at over here. You're made fun of because it's not paid well."[39]

School life in India can vary dramatically, depending on the school being attended. For instance, some schools have modern classrooms, lots of teachers, and plenty of supplies, including technology such as computers for the students to use. Twelve-year-old Diya and ten-year-old Naina attend a modern school in the city of Delhi. Their school day goes from 8:30 a.m. to 2:30 p.m. In addition to the regular school subjects such as reading, math, and writing, they have classes in art, PE, yoga, Western music, and Indian music. They also are served lunch at school. Their mother describes their lunch as "strictly vegetarian and mostly Indian. A dal [a dish made from lentils, peas, or beans], rice, veggie and rotis (Indian bread) with a sweet (ice cream or kheer) or a fruit is the usual menu. They need special permission for home-food. My younger daughter carries a 'tiffin' (snack) to school which they have around 10am."[40]

In contrast, some schools have no money even for basic necessities such as desks, chairs, and electricity. Eleven-year-old Kiran lives in the village of Sultanpur, near the city of New Delhi. She sits on the floor at school. "My feet goes off to sleep sometimes, and I lose track of the class," she says. "A desk and a chair would be very nice."[41] Because schools such as this have limited funds with which to pay teachers, a classroom

can have more than fifty students. Another common problem in schools with limited funds is an absence of toilets for students to use. Ten-year-old Golu Kumari, who attends a school in the country, says that at her school, students are forced to go to the bathroom outside, which can be embarrassing. "When we had to relieve ourselves, we wouldn't go because we were afraid the boys would follow us," she says. "They would stand there and watch us."[42]

Regardless of whether they sit at desks or on the floor, boys and girls are typically separated from one another in school. Often, boys and girls attend separate schools. In schools that do have both sexes, teachers usually strive to limit contact between them. Student Shourjomoy Ghosh says, "Even in co-ed schools, you have rules that demand that boys and girls cannot sit together. The excuse that is given for this is that having students of the other gender in a class would be a 'distraction.'"[43] According to a 2015 story in the *Huffington Post*, Pallikoodam, a coed school in Kerala, has a rule that boys and girls must maintain a distance of 3.3 feet (1 m) from one another.

Exams

No matter what type of school they attend, most Indian youths complain about their secondary school exams. These exams test students in a number of subjects, including math, science, and social studies. The exams are extremely rigorous, and students often study day and night for weeks to prepare for them. Most students report that the exams are extremely stressful and that their parents place a tremendous amount of pressure on them to do well in school so that they can get a good job in the future. In fact, research shows that many Indian parents believe that a successful career is the most important goal in life for their children.

Exams are so important that young people who fail them often report that their lives become miserable and that their friends and family ridicule and chastise them. For instance, Vijay Prasad lives in the city of Chennai. He says, "I failed in my 10th [grade] board exams. . . . When the results were out it was like as if the sky had fallen on my head. I was ashamed to go out anywhere of the fear of being ridiculed by friends."[44] Jorawar Singh failed his twelfth-grade exams. He says:

> "Even in co-ed schools, you have rules that demand that boys and girls cannot sit together. The excuse that is given for this is that having students of the other gender in a class would be a 'distraction.'"[43]
>
> —Shourjomoy Ghosh, a student in India

What is it like to fail in the 12th grade? My question to you is, which country do you stay in? If it's India, you'd be better off [committing] a murder. Because that's where I am from. Please don't get me wrong here. May be I am exaggerating but that's because I have had 3x of failing once academically. But if you fail 12th people, you will feel like that mosquito who was sitting on a wall and all of a sudden was turned into a caligraphy of blood and twisted legs with a single thud of a chappal (slipper). You would be looked down upon, nagged, nailed, told you would have less of a future than you would have had if [you] had fallen in the zones passing with flying colours.[45]

Because there is so much pressure to do well on exams and be accepted into a good school, some students resort to cheating. There is evidence that cheating is common practice in many schools and is often encouraged by parents and tolerated by teachers. Craig Jeffrey is a professor of development geography at the University of Oxford. He talked to students in India about the prevalence of cheating. Pratap Singh, a university student in the northern state of Uttar Pradesh, told him, "Cheating happens at every level. Students bribe to get admission and good results. Research students get professors to write their dissertations. And the professors cheat too, publishing articles in bogus journals."[46]

Call Center Jobs

One common job for Indian college graduates is working in a call center. In these centers they spend their time on the telephone, handling customer service calls from countries such as the United States and Great Britain. These jobs exist because many companies in these and other countries outsource their customer service to places where labor is cheaper, including India. The pay is relatively good in India's call centers; however, the work is fast paced and repetitive, and it often involves dealing with unhappy customers. Further, in order to speak with customers who live in different time zones, employees must often work at night.

As a result, many call center employees report that their jobs can be stressful. Abhijnan Nath, who lives in Bengaluru, explains, "The challenge lies not only conforming to the time and speech of their customers but also handling irate and angry callers. The repetitive nature of the job and repeated rejections from clients are key factors that dishearten the Indian call center employees." Despite the stress though, these jobs remain popular because they pay well compared to many of the other jobs available to college graduates.

Abhijnan Nath, comment on Quora, "What Is It Like to Work in a Call Center in India?," August 29, 2012. www.quora.com.

Pinki Singh, another college student in Uttar Pradesh, says that by not cheating, she was actually in the minority. "If you really want to know the truth," she says, "there's no point in studying properly. You just need to buy one of the cheat books sold in the bazaar and learn the answers. In my first year doing history I tried to study properly, but my seniors just told me: 'Buy the cheat books.'"[47] In 2015 reporters published photographs of Indian parents in the state of Bihar climbing the walls of a four-story school to pass crib sheets to their children so that they could cheat on their board exams. The publicity highlighted the fact that much of the cheating taking place is condoned or even initiated by parents.

> "There's no point in studying properly. You just need to buy one of the cheat books sold in the bazaar and learn the answers."[47]
>
> —Pinki Singh, a college student in Uttar Pradesh

Job Prospects

In the early 2000s, research showed that a significant percentage of India's young people were not attending school; however, since then the country has made numerous efforts to improve these statistics. The country has built more schools, hired more teachers, and persuaded more parents of the importance of sending their children to school. As a result, more young people than ever before are attending school and graduating from college, and an increasing percentage of the world's college graduates are coming from India.

However, this growing number of graduates has also been problematic because there are not enough jobs in India for the millions of young people who graduate every year. In 2016 the *Times of India* published a story that illustrates just how many graduates are unable to find a job. The municipality of Amroha in Uttar Pradesh advertised vacancies for 114 positions. Of these jobs, the story says, "The posts do not require educational qualifications because the work involves manual labour like cleaning streets with brooms, maintaining drainage and municipal sewer lines." However, in response to the advertisement, the municipality was inundated with nineteen thousand applications, many of them from college graduates, some even with advanced degrees. Nakul Singh, who has a bachelor's degree in science, says, "I have been jobless since I finished college in 2014. So when I heard about openings as sweepers, I thought this would be a good opportunity for me to earn a living and help my family."[48]

India's Ministry of Human Resource Development worries that another reason that college graduates are having trouble finding jobs is that many universities are not providing their students with a high standard of education. In a 2016 report, the ministry discusses university ratings under the government-established accreditation system. The report states:

> Of the 140 universities accredited by the National Assessment and Accreditation Council (NAAC), only 32 percent are rated as A grade. Among the 2,780 colleges accredited by the NAAC, only 9 percent are rated as A grade. Among the accredited institutions, 68 percent of the universities and 91 percent of the colleges are rated average or below average in terms of the quality parameters specified by the NAAC.[49]

Unemployed educated women register at an employment office in Allahabad. Although more and more young people are attending college in India, there are not enough jobs for the millions who graduate every year.

The ministry concludes that as a result of the poor performance of these universities, many students do not have employable skills when they graduate.

Child Labor

While many youths complain that they have trouble finding a job after they graduate, some face a different problem, and are forced to go to work while they are still children. A significant number of Indian young people spend their days working rather than attending school. According to the *CIA World Factbook*, about 12 percent of India's children ages five to fourteen work. UNICEF estimates that overall, about 10.2 million children work in India. Many labor in the fields doing things such as tending livestock or harvesting crops. Child laborers also work in urban areas, performing tasks such as making matches, cigarettes, and saris; weaving carpets; laboring in hotels and restaurants; and working as servants in the homes of the middle class or wealthy. Widespread child labor is the result of widespread poverty; most of the children who work do so to help their families earn enough money for food and other basic necessities.

> "When my grandfather died, my parents had no other choice but to borrow money. We became debt-bonded. The owner used to make me work the whole day, forcibly."[50]
>
> —Puran, who worked as a child laborer in India

Fourteen-year-old Puran Banjara and thirteen-year-old Samsur Mohamad both worked as child laborers in India. They later spoke about their experiences to help raise awareness about the issue. "I was breaking stones with my brother," says Banjara. "When my grandfather died, my parents had no other choice but to borrow money. We became debt-bonded. The owner used to make me work the whole day, forcibly. I didn't feel like working. I never saw any books during my childhood. Both of my parents are illiterate."[50] Mohamad says, "I used to collect garbage with my two brothers. We used [to] go through the garbage fields to look for glass, plastic and other recyclable materials. We collected about 10 rupees [equivalent of about 16 cents] for each bag."[51]

A six-year-old girl picks cotton in southern India. Child labor is rampant due to widespread poverty, with about 10 million children working to help their families afford basic necessities.

Illiteracy

Young people who are unable to attend school because they are working, among other reasons, often end up illiterate. Overall, illiteracy is a significant problem in India. In its 2016 report, the Ministry of Human Resource Development states that only about 86 percent of youths ages fifteen to twenty-four are literate, and the country has the largest number of illiterate youths in the world. Mission India, a religious organization, discusses illiteracy in the north Indian state of Bihar. It explains that Bihar is the most illiterate state, with 32 million illiterate people. Nearly 20 million of these are women, and the organization explains that their illiteracy makes their lives difficult in many ways. The organization says:

> They can't read a bus schedule or labels on a medicine bottle. They can't write a letter to family living in another area. These women can't count change at the market, or even know if they are being cheated by unscrupulous vendors. And they can't help their children with their homework or read a bedtime story. Illiteracy touches every single moment of their day . . . and they have little hope of a different future.[52]

However, India is working to change this situation, and illiteracy rates are actually lower than they were in the past.

Absenteeism Among Teachers

A relatively common problem in Indian schools is that students arrive at school and find that there is no teacher to instruct them. This is because there is a high rate of absenteeism among Indian teachers. A 2013 report from Transparency International, an organization that campaigns against corruption, states that on average, Indian teachers miss class almost 25 percent of the time. The report explains that there are various reasons for absenteeism, ranging from legitimate ones such as teachers having to care for sick relatives to illegitimate ones such as teachers working other jobs when they are scheduled to teach. Manoj Mishra is a district education officer in the state of Uttar Pradesh, where he investigates teacher truancy. A 2016 *New York Times* article relates some of his findings. Mishra found that absenteeism was common; in fact, some absent teachers actually lived nowhere near the schools they were supposed to teach in and bribed others into reporting them present. Unfortunately, in many of India's schools—particularly in rural areas—when teachers are absent, no substitutes are available, and student learning suffers.

Even though India has continued to make significant improvements to its education system in recent years, challenges remain. The Ministry of Human Resource Development stresses that every year, the education system prepares a huge number of young people for India's workforce, and these young people will be the ones who guide India in the future. As a result, it points out, the quality of education in India is vitally important to the country's future. It says, "India is one of the youngest nations in the world with more than 54 percent of its total population below 25 years of age. This necessitates that the youth in the country are equipped with the skills and knowledge to enter the workforce through education and training."[53]

CHAPTER FOUR

Social Life

Socializing and friendship are essential to young people in India. Just as Indians believe it is very important to spend time with and show loyalty to their families, they also believe in the importance of having strong friendships. Lalit Singh Rajput lives in Uttar Pradesh. He explains that Indian youths form very close friendships with one another and will always help one another. He says, "When you are in problem or on your back they will leave no stone unturned to help you and praise you."[54] Youths form these friendships by spending much of their free time socializing together at one another's homes, the movies, the mall, restaurants, parks, and other public spaces.

Relationships Between Young People

Like young people all over the world, Indian young people report that in addition to having close platonic friendships, they think a lot about dating and sex. However, most Indian parents remain very conservative when it comes to these topics. They decide whom their children will marry and strongly disapprove of their having sex or even dating before marriage. One way that traditional parents try to prevent any type of romantic relationship before marriage is by keeping their children from interacting with members of the opposite sex after they reach puberty. Shreehari K U, who lives in the south of India, explains, "In our society, there is an imaginary line that blocks the interaction between a boy and a girl after a certain age. This is called the 'Volatile' stage wherein the boy and girl starts to mature. I recollect my mom saying 'you've grown up now, don't play with girls to much!" He says that he was even discouraged from corresponding with his own cousin, explaining, "Recently my aunt saw a conversation between me and my distant cousin on WhatsApp. She started asking me awkward question related to it. . . . And I was like 'this is my cousin sister aunty, why thinking bad about it too?'"[55]

Despite the fact that parents often work hard to discourage young people from having relationships or dating, Indian young people commonly report that they do date—they simply do it in secret. Journalist Nita J. Kulkarni, who lives in India, says that dating has become widespread there, whether or not parents approve. She explains, "Parental disapproval and society's contempt often drives friendship and romance with the opposite sex underground! Boys and girls from even traditional families are dating but secrecy is the name of the game." She gives the example of eighteen-year-old Rohit and his sixteen-year-old girlfriend, who both come from conservative families and are keeping their relationship a secret: "They usually seek out deserted movie halls or unknown cafes while both their parents are under the impression that they are out in a group. Their group covers for them. Love letters and cards are exchanged through common friends, and calls are made from cells."[56]

> "Parental disapproval and society's contempt often drives friendship and romance with the opposite sex underground!"[56]
>
> —Nita J. Kulkarni, a journalist living in India

Although most young people who have relationships with the opposite sex do so in secret, there is a growing number of youths in India's cities who do not need to be so secretive because their parents actually allow them to have opposite-sex friends and even to date. Rima Patel comments, "Things are changing very quickly. Parents are allowing their kids to go out and do things that they weren't able to do; they want them to have the fun they didn't."[57]

Although attitudes toward sex remain largely conservative, even among young people, many Indian youths report that they have had premarital sex. Estimates vary widely, but many experts believe that overall, premarital sex has become increasingly common in India. Clinical psychologist Seema Hingorrany says, "In the last five years I have seen the number [of young people

Young women hang out together in Kumbakonam in southeast India. Many parents discourage their children from making friends with those of the opposite sex after puberty.

having sex] rise rapidly. Around 50–75 per cent young girls and guys lose their virginity much before they are anywhere near adulthood."[58] In the HT-MaRS Youth Survey, a 2014 survey of 5,214 urban youths ages eighteen to twenty-five, 63 percent of eighteen- to twenty-one-year-olds said they believe that premarital sex is permissible. Despite these numbers, however, many young people in India—particularly young men—paradoxically want to marry a virgin. Avneesh Murgai, a fine arts student from Delhi, explains, "We are westernised enough to indulge in a casual sexual encounter but still caught in the patriarchal time warp where we cannot entertain the idea of our wife/girlfriend ever being touched by another man."[59] The re-

> "Around 50–75 per cent young girls and guys lose their virginity much before they are anywhere near adulthood."[58]
>
> —Seema Hingorrany, a clinical psychologist

sult is that most young people keep their sexual experiences a secret.

Close Male Friendships

Although Indian society usually discourages close physical contact between young people of the opposite sex and views it as sexual, it is common to see close physical contact between young men. In many Western countries, such as the United States, when two males touch one another, people usually view it as sexualized; however, this is not the case in India. Ashish Gupta, who lives

Eve Teasing

While many Indians have conservative attitudes toward sex, it is very common for men and boys to sexually harass females with something called "Eve teasing." Eve teasing is attention in the form of stares, comments, whistles, and even flashing or physical molestation. The term is related to a story in the Bible, in which the woman Eve tempted Adam into eating the apple that God had forbidden them to eat. Many Indians see it as innocent fun, and many girls simply brush this attention and harassment off as an annoying but unavoidable part of life.

However, Eve teasing is not always experienced as a harmless inconvenience. Sometimes it turns into sexual assault and causes lasting harm to girls and women. Ambika Kohli grew up in Delhi. She says that Eve teasing is extremely common. Kohli explains:

Most of my friends at some stage of their lives (even at the age of 5 and 6) have experienced sexual harassment in forms of unwanted sexual contacts, unwanted intercourse, unwanted touching, sexist comments, or gestures given by men and boys. . . . I myself have experienced such incidences endless time that I can write a whole book on it (I am only 28 years). Sometimes I ignored, sometimes I fought back, and once I got acutely scared because I was only 11 years old at that time.

Kohli says that sexual harassment is so common that although girls and young women rarely forget the experiences, most try to ignore it so that they can get on with their lives.

Ambika Kohli, "Eve-Teasing a Normal Stress for Delhi's Girls?," Project MonMa. http://projectmonma.co.

in India, explains, "Because in India holding hands is culturally not considered anything to do with sexual orientation. It's merely way of showing affection, bonding, and camaraderie that all men, women and children do. However, holding hands by people of opposite sex is considered sign of romantic involvement."[60]

Lalit Singh Rajput explains that in addition to holding hands, Indian youths can spend time together without being assumed to be homosexual, as they might be in other countries. He says:

> In foreign countries you have to have some important task at hand (like meetings, party etc) to meet your fellow male friends but in india it can be just a tafri walk [slang for idle fun] on roadside or eating golgappe [common street snack] or meeting at local theka [liquor shop] (best of all) or can be no reason also. Neither you nor your friend nor anyone around will feel or say anything awkward. Afterall its our way of life.[61]

Sports and Board Games

In addition to spending time with their friends, many Indian youths play sports in their free time. Cricket is the most popular sport in India, and it is very common to see young people playing the game in public parks and open spaces. India also has a national team that is extremely popular. In 2011 the country won the Cricket World Cup for the first time since 1983, and people all over the country were so excited that they filled the streets in wild celebration. Many partied all night long.

Podcaster and columnist Subash Jayaraman talks about how popular cricket is among boys in India. He says that they often use whatever they can find to make balls and wickets:

> Balls could be hard tennis balls, cork balls, taped tennis balls, rubber balls, or those made with cycle tyre tubes. Stumps could be twigs, chairs, schoolbags, bricks, or three lines drawn on a wall. . . . I was around 11 when cricket took hold of almost all my waking hours. Every opportunity to get together with my friends in the neighbourhood cen-

tred on impromptu games. . . . My evenings, weekends, holidays and vacations were spent playing cricket in the streets, in the little area by the town's flour mill, on old fort grounds and on terraces.[62]

In addition to cricket, a number of other sports are popular, including field hockey, soccer, and badminton. Indian young people also like to play kabaddi, a contact sport that originated in ancient India. It is often described as a mixture of tag and wrestling. In this game there are two teams. A raider from one team must take a deep breath and run into the opponent's court, where he or she must tag as many opponents as possible, and return to his or her side without being caught. All this must be done within that one breath, with the raider chanting "kabaddi," so that the referee knows that he or she has not inhaled. Kabaddi has become increasingly popular in recent years. It is widely reported to have become the second-most watched sport in India after cricket.

Kabaddi is so popular that India has national men's and women's teams and competes in international competitions. Many

Friends play cricket—the most popular sport in India—in a public field in Maharashtra.

young people aspire to be on those teams one day. However, for girls it is more challenging to turn those dreams into reality because many traditional parents believe the sport is not appropriate for females. Tejaswini Bai and Mamta Poojari are both on the national team, and they explain that their parents initially discouraged them from playing. Poojari says:

> My parents were against me playing kabbadi because it involves a lot of physical action. We get injured every day. And as a kid, when I started playing, I didn't know how to guard myself from injuries. So, I would return home with lots of bruises. My parents told me that I can't play this sport as my skin was getting damaged. To top it, we had to wear shorts and play . . . my family had a problem with that too.[63]

Bai agrees, saying that her parents were skeptical at first because they saw kabaddi as a man's sport. However, she says that they eventually accepted it, and now they even allow her younger sister to play too.

In addition to sports, Indian youths enjoy playing board games. Chess, which is believed to have originated in India, is one of the most popular of these games and has become increasingly popular among young people in recent years. Chess is taught in a growing number of schools, and many parents sign their children up for chess clubs. For instance, Dhananjay Ramraje, who runs the Chanakya Chess Club in Mumbai, says, "We get as many as 50 calls a day from interested parents."[64] Shubangi Tekukar explains why she likes her four-year-old daughter, Aadva, to play chess: "It is a game in which there are many moves and out of that you choose one best move. Like that, in your life also chess helps to improve your ability to make the best decisions."[65] In addition to playing in clubs, children who play chess also have the ability to compete in the many chess tournaments that occur across the country. Those who become chess champions are often widely celebrated. For example, Viswanathan Anand, who at age eighteen became India's first grandmaster—the highest rank awarded by the World Chess Federation—is a well-known celebrity in India.

Movies and Television

Watching movies and television is another favorite pastime among Indian young people. According to statistics portal Statista, the country is the largest movie producer in the world, releasing more than one thousand films each year. Statista reports that in 2015 more than 2 billion movie tickets were sold in India, making it the leading film market in the world. The most popular type of films produced are Hindi-language films created in the city of Mumbai. The film industry there has been nicknamed Bollywood, a play on the word *Hollywood*. Bollywood films usually have numerous elaborate song-and-dance routines, and romantic drama is common. The songs from Bollywood movies are so popular that they go on sale months before the movie is released. This means that although not all young people watch Bollywood films, they usually know the songs from the films.

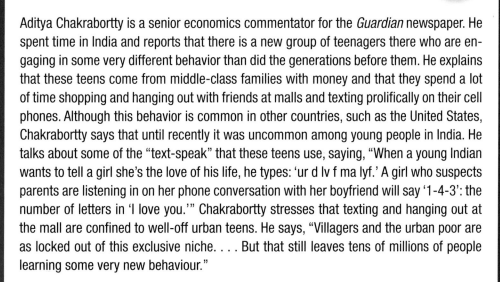

Middle-Class Teens

Aditya Chakrabortty is a senior economics commentator for the *Guardian* newspaper. He spent time in India and reports that there is a new group of teenagers there who are engaging in some very different behavior than did the generations before them. He explains that these teens come from middle-class families with money and that they spend a lot of time shopping and hanging out with friends at malls and texting prolifically on their cell phones. Although this behavior is common in other countries, such as the United States, Chakrabortty says that until recently it was uncommon among young people in India. He talks about some of the "text-speak" that these teens use, saying, "When a young Indian wants to tell a girl she's the love of his life, he types: 'ur d lv f ma lyf.' A girl who suspects parents are listening in on her phone conversation with her boyfriend will say '1-4-3': the number of letters in 'I love you.'" Chakrabortty stresses that texting and hanging out at the mall are confined to well-off urban teens. He says, "Villagers and the urban poor are as locked out of this exclusive niche. . . . But that still leaves tens of millions of people learning some very new behaviour."

Aditya Chakrabortty, "Hanging Out with India's First Real Teenagers," *Guardian* (Manchester), March 29, 2011. www.the guardian.com.

Though going to the movies is a popular pastime, many young people—for instance the very poor or people in rural areas—cannot afford to go to the theater or have no access to one, so they watch television. Partho Dasgupta, chief executive officer of Broadcast Audience Research Council India, a company that analyzes television viewing, comments that watching movies and television shows is a way of life. "Nothing binds an Indian family together like a television set," he says. "Community watching is in our DNA, and this is across urban and rural India. We love laughing, crying and celebrating together."[66] According to Dasgupta, 83 percent of households in urban areas own a television. The percentage in rural areas is much lower at 40 percent, but still relatively high considering the huge number of people who live in poverty.

No matter where they live, Indian youths are usually able to find a place to watch television. Blogger Julie spent thirteen months traveling around the world with her husband and two children. Her trip included India. She talks about touring the Dharavi slum, Mumbai's largest. She says that walking through the dark alleys and glancing into the tiny homes there, she noticed that while most people did not own very much at all, many did have televisions. She recalls, "Every fifteen feet there would be a doorway leading into a house, a singular 4×4 meter room which was the kitchen, living room, and bedroom for an entire family. People would be laying on the floor watching TV."[67] Kavya Guddehithulu Nagesh, who lives in India, comments on television in rural areas:

> TV is very important part of life: Life mostly here is very quiet or rather dull. Don't get me wrong but people hardly go out after dusk. The day's routine is over after 7. There are no malls, hangout places or theatres. There is not much to look forward. Every villager is eager to watch the gos-

> "Nothing binds an Indian family together like a television set. . . . Community watching is in our DNA, and this is across urban and rural India. We love laughing, crying and celebrating together."[66]
>
> —Partho Dasgupta, chief executive officer of Broadcast Audience Research Council India

sip, current affairs, movies etc. Its not only their source of entertainment but also serves as topic of discussion for next few days. Not every house gets newspaper but every house has TV. TV here is a very powerful media here.[68]

Cell Phones and Social Media

While watching movies and television is a common pastime for Indian young people, the use of cell phones is still relatively rare. Only a small number of Indian youths have their own cell phones or use social media. In fact, according to a 2015 report by research company We Are Social, barely 10 percent of the entire population is active on social media. For the majority of India's young people, socializing still takes place in person, not over social networks or via cell phone.

Muslim youths take a selfie in front of the seventeenth-century Jama Masjid, a mosque in Delhi. The use of cell phones and social media is steadily growing among teens in India.

However, the number of teens who use cell phones and social media, though small, is steadily increasing. Most of these teens belong to upper- or middle-class families. And like teens all over the world, those teens who do own cell phones use them constantly. Aditya Chakrabortty, senior economics commentator for the *Guardian*, spent some time hanging out with a group of middle-class teens at a mall in Kolkata and reports that their cell phone use was prolific. He says, "Everyone on my table at the Forum claimed to send and receive more than 1,000 texts a day, having to delete their entire inboxes every night."[69] In addition to texting one another, many teens who have cell phones use them to access social media. A 2016 study by Fortis Healthcare revealed that when Indian teens use social media, they are greatly influenced by it. Researchers surveyed 1,350 young people, ages fourteen to seventeen, who live in Delhi. They report, "The impact of the media on these young minds is actually staggering."[70] For instance, of those young people surveyed, 74 percent thought that social media is the best source for information and facts.

Whether they own cell phones and use social media or live in the slums and crowd around a television with two other families, Indian youths are like youths all over the world. They love to spend time with friends, are interested in dating and sex—even if it is forbidden by their parents—and enjoy watching television and playing sports.

CHAPTER FIVE

Religion

The country of India is rich with religious tradition. It is believed that four of the world's major religions—Buddhism, Jainism, Hinduism, and Sikhism—originated there. Hinduism is the most common religion in India and is followed by an estimated 80 percent of the population. But India is also home to substantial populations of people who practice other major religions, including Islam, Christianity, Zoroastrianism, and Judaism. In fact, India has one of the largest Muslim populations in the world. Stanley Wolpert teaches Indian history at the University of California, Los Angeles, and is the author of several books about India. He states that Indians believe that religion has real power in everyday life. He explains, "To Indians, in general, religion and philosophy are mother's milk, daily nourishment, not esoterica to be remembered only on Saturdays or Sundays, locked in books never read. Most Indians believe that the gods and stars affect everyone's fate, today, tomorrow, all part of the cosmic balance."[71]

Hinduism

A child who is born a Hindu grows up celebrating important moments in his or her life through Hindu ritual. These begin at birth and continue throughout life. One of the first is the naming ceremony, which usually takes place on the twelfth day after birth. Although the ceremony varies, in many cases friends and family bring gifts for the baby and parents, and a priest says prayers and blesses the infant.

There are also ceremonies to celebrate the first time the baby eats solid food, his or her first haircut, and his or her becoming old enough to attend school. Most Hindus observe the ritual of the first haircut, which usually occurs at about a year of age. Hindus believe that the hair with which a baby is born is connected with its past life and is thus impure, so that hair is shaved off to purify the baby and ensure his or her well-being for the future. One writer describes this ceremony:

> The mother sits with the child in her lap and faces the west of the sacred fire. The priest shaves off a part of the child's hair while chanting sacred hymns. After that, the barber shaves off the rest of the hair. In some families, the father performs the initial rite instead of the priest. The shaven head is washed with holy water (*Gangajal*). Then a paste of turmeric and sandalwood is applied. It is believed that this mixture cools the head and speeds up the healing of any nicks and cuts. The shaved hair is either offered to a deity or to a sacred river like the Ganga.[72]

In addition to observing various milestones, Hindus celebrate numerous holidays and festivals throughout the year. Young people enjoy taking part in these festivals, which are usually joyous affairs. One favorite of young people is Holi, also known as the Festival of Color, which celebrates the arrival of spring. One of the most fun parts of Holi is when people crowd into public spaces and throw handfuls of colored powder over one another while simultaneously getting drenched with water. National Public Radio contributor Chhavi Sachdev remembers the joy of Holi as a child, saying:

> When I was growing up in New Delhi, Holi . . . [meant] waking up early to fill and knot a gazillion water balloons; wearing my oldest clothes and then traveling in roving groups trying to outdo each other in pelting water balloons—shivering in our wet clothes, smearing ink and *pakka*, or powdered colors, all over friends and enemies, followed by an hour in the shower trying in vain to scrub the colors off. Everyone showed up at school the next day sporting various shades of green, blue and silver.[73]

Young people dance in the street during Holi, also known as the Festival of Color, a popular Hindu holiday that celebrates the arrival of spring.

The Caste System

One religious tradition that has a strong effect on everyday life is the concept of caste. It comes from the Hindu religion, and it has been an important part of India's culture for hundreds of years. Under the traditional caste system, there is a hierarchy of four different castes. At the highest level are the Brahmins, who are intellectuals, teachers, and spiritual leaders. Next are the Kshatriyas, who are the warriors and princes. The Vaishyas—merchants and traders—are third, and the Shudras, who are servants and manual laborers, are fourth. In addition to these four castes, another group evolved within the system. The people in this group, often called the untouchables, perform all of the jobs that would cause impurity to the higher castes, including doing laundry, working with leather (which comes from a dead animal), butchering animals, and collecting garbage. Although they were called untouchables for many years, the people in this group resented that name and recently renamed themselves the Dalits, which means "the oppressed."

In 1950 the government implemented a constitutional provision that made it illegal to discriminate by caste. But in reality a large number of Indians continue to follow the caste system, and thus caste continues to have a major impact on the everyday lives of many Indians. Many people remain extremely conscious of the caste that they, and those around them, belong to and hold on to the belief that people should not be allowed to marry into a higher caste or take a job that has traditionally been the domain of a higher caste. This often makes it difficult for people to break out of the caste that they were born into. For example, Ovindra Pal, who

Religious Texts in School

Many Indian young people study Hindu religious texts in school. For example, some read the *Mahabharata*, an epic narrative about ancient India that also contains philosophical and religious elements. Some people are opposed to this practice, arguing that teaching religious material in public school is a violation of the constitution. However, others insist that while these texts do have religious elements, they also teach students about Indian culture and history. Anil K. Rajvanshi runs the Nimbkar Agricultural Research Institute. He explains:

> Slowly and silently we are moving towards a time when we will completely forget our great Indian stories, tales and culture. . . . The folk tales of India from all states, from our great books like the *Ramayana*, *Mahabharata*, *Panchatantra* etc. should be taught in schools to inspire the children. There is a great wisdom in these books which needs to be distilled and presented in a form which can be easily understood by students.

Anil K. Rajvanshi, "Why Indian Classics Should Be Taught in Our Schools," *Huffington Post*, July 15, 2016. www.huffingtonpost.com.

lives in the town of Meerut, says that despite graduating from college with a master's degree, he ended up skinning dead cows for a living because that is what his Dalit family was expected to do. His sons are also pursuing university degrees, and he hopes that they will be the generation to finally break away from the pressure of the caste system. He says, "One of my sons is a law graduate from Delhi University. The other is pursuing engineering from the Indian Institute of Information Technology, Allahabad. . . . Mine will be the last generation from my family to skin cows."[74]

Upasana Chauhan also talks about how the caste system has affected her life. She says that she grew up in a town in the Indian state of Haryana and that she was constantly reminded that she had to marry someone of the same caste. She says, "Do not fall in love with somebody who does not belong to our caste. Of all the rules I had to follow as a girl, this was the most important."[75]

Discrimination based on caste is most common in the case of the Dalits, who are estimated to make up almost a fifth of India's population. For instance, in many villages, the Dalits are forced to live in a separate area and are kept from using the village well or shopping in certain stores because the rest of the village is afraid that contact with Dalits will make them impure.

> "Do not fall in love with somebody who does not belong to our caste. Of all the rules I had to follow as a girl, this was the most important."[75]
>
> —Upasana Chauhan, a resident of Haryana, India

Sukhadeo Thorat is a professor of economics at Jawaharlal Nehru University and chair of the Indian Council of Social Science Research in New Delhi. Nidhi Sadana Sabharwal is a principal research fellow at the Indian Institute of Dalit Studies in New Delhi. They discuss how Dalit children are discriminated against in an Indian classroom:

The pain is perceptible in nine-year-old Shankar's voice as he recounts how he's made to sit at the back of the class with other children from a similar "low caste" group. He says his teacher doesn't wish to accidentally touch them, keeping them as far away as possible from the rest of the children. His peers from the "upper caste" call him an "untouchable"; when he complains to the teachers, they see no issue. "You are untouchable—what else should they call you?" His sister, who is 8, is asked to clean the classroom—that's her task because she's a girl and an "untouchable." At lunch, Shankar says the children from the other castes are served food provided by the government, while his fellow caste children are asked to wait outside the classroom; should any food remain after the teachers and "upper caste" children have eaten, it may then be offered to Shankar and other children from the "lower castes."[76]

A Dalit woman sells statues in Mumbai. Although it is illegal to discriminate by caste, people from low castes, particularly the Dalits, face ongoing prejudice in their day-to-day lives.

Reincarnation

Related to the idea of caste is the Hindu belief in reincarnation, which also has a strong impact on how young people grow up in India. Hindus believe that when people die, they are reincarnated, which means they come back to life in another form. Hindus also believe that all of a person's actions throughout life influence that rebirth; if a person has lived a good life—for example, respecting the gods—he or she will be reborn in a higher caste. A person who has not lived a good life will be reborn in a lower caste or maybe even as an animal. In some religions, people believe that if they are good, they will go to heaven or some type of paradise after they die, but Hindus do not share a similar belief. Instead, the ultimate goal is to transcend human life. It is believed that if a person lives a perfect life, he or she will finally be released from the cycle of death and rebirth.

Stanley Wolpert explains that because of the belief in reincarnation, many young people are taught to passively accept the status they are born into as a result of their own actions, and thus something they deserve. He asks, "How could any Untouchable possibly complain, after all, about his lowly position in life? Surely he must have done many dastardly deeds in previous lives. . . . Now his own Karma was punishing him."[77] In addition, belief in reincarnation means that many people not only passively accept their status but strive to fulfill their role in the community to the best of their ability so they can be reborn into a better position. Wolpert says, "An Untouchable could rise to Brahmanic heights of goodness and glory, but *only* by being a perfect Untouchable first! One must do one's duty without complaint, without hesitation, or doubt, or grudging, with no silent or vocal contempt."[78] As a result of such beliefs, some young people never strive to improve their condition in life.

Homosexual and Transgender Youths

Hindu beliefs also affect social attitudes toward homosexual and transgender people. Many Indians believe that homosexuality goes against the Hindu religion, and this view of homosexuality as an unnatural behavior is even reflected in India's laws. The Indian Penal Code makes homosexuality a criminal offense. It states, "Whoever voluntarily has carnal intercourse against the order of nature with any man, woman or animal, shall be punished with imprisonment for life, or with imprisonment of either description for a term which may extend to 10 years, and shall also be liable to fine."[79] Though homosexuals are rarely arrested for breaking this law, many report that they face widespread disapproval, and their lives are often difficult. Commenting online, an anonymous writer shares his experiences:

> It is very difficult to be a gay in India. That can be very depressing. It includes all kinds of bullying, teasing right from the school, where boys always try to make fun of you because of your feminine expressions in your speech, composure and habits. This is not just limited to bullying by just boys[;] even teachers, other elders make fun of you. Even with you learning how to hide it through time by good imitating and practice, inside it will be very killing that one or other person in your college or university always identifies it and keeps an eye on you.[80]

In contrast to its treatment of homosexuals, India has recently become much more accepting of transgender youths, an attitude that is also rooted in the Hindu religion. In 2014 the Indian Supreme Court made a ruling that recognizes transgender people and gives them the same legal rights as everybody else. Under the court's decision, India has created a third gender of people that includes transgender people, eunuchs, and those people who have both male and female anatomy. These people can identify as this third gender on all legal documents.

"It is very difficult to be a gay in India. That can be very depressing. It includes all kinds of bullying, teasing right from the school, where boys always try to make fun of you."[80]

—Anonymous writer

In 2014 the *Times of India* reported that in the first official census that includes this third gender, about 490,000 people were counted in the category. A significant number of these were children, showing that many parents have embraced the recognition of the third gender. Rajesh Sampath is an assistant professor of the philosophy of justice, rights, and social change at Brandeis

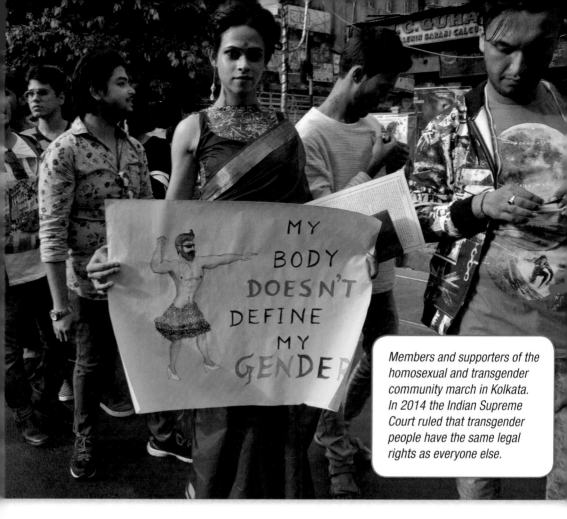

My
Body
Doesn't
Define
My
Gender

Members and supporters of the homosexual and transgender community march in Kolkata. In 2014 the Indian Supreme Court ruled that transgender people have the same legal rights as everyone else.

University. He explains how the court decision was strongly influenced by the Hindu religion:

> To provide support for its legal defense of the third gender, the Indian Supreme Court drew from ancient moral-philosophical classics of Hinduism. In one cited epic, the *Mahabharata*, a prince's death wish is to marry, but no one would accept the offer of a dying prince. And so Lord Krishna, a male deity, descends to earth in the form of a woman named Mohini to marry to him. This and other stories provide divine justification for transgenderism, even according them supernatural status.[81]

Transgender people all over India celebrated the 2014 court decision, optimistic that it will make their lives much easier.

Religion and Food

Another part of life that is affected by religion in India is diet. Some of India's religions prohibit or discourage certain foods. For instance, Muslims believe that pork is unclean, and their religion prohibits them from eating it. Hindus do not eat beef, because they believe that cows are sacred. Cows are often treated with such respect that they are allowed to wander in the streets, getting in the way of traffic and becoming a nuisance. Beyond their reverence for cows, Hindus believe that all creatures are worthy of compassion and respect, so many Hindus are vegetarians. While food varies widely by region, most Indian food contains a lot of spices and vegetables. Meals are usually served with flatbread or rice. People often eat with their hands and share dishes.

Jainism is another religion whose followers eat vegetarian food. Like Hinduism, this religion is founded on nonviolence; however, Jains believe in nonviolence even toward plants. As a result, not only are they vegetarian, they do not eat anything that grows underground—such as potatoes or garlic—because

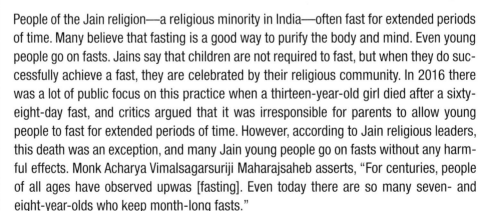

Jainism and Fasting

People of the Jain religion—a religious minority in India—often fast for extended periods of time. Many believe that fasting is a good way to purify the body and mind. Even young people go on fasts. Jains say that children are not required to fast, but when they do successfully achieve a fast, they are celebrated by their religious community. In 2016 there was a lot of public focus on this practice when a thirteen-year-old girl died after a sixty-eight-day fast, and critics argued that it was irresponsible for parents to allow young people to fast for extended periods of time. However, according to Jain religious leaders, this death was an exception, and many Jain young people go on fasts without any harmful effects. Monk Acharya Vimalsagarsuriji Maharajsaheb asserts, "For centuries, people of all ages have observed upwas [fasting]. Even today there are so many seven- and eight-year-olds who keep month-long fasts."

Quoted in *Times of India*, "Girl's Death After Fast Sparks Debate Among Jains," October 11, 2016. http://timesofindia .indiatimes.com.

they believe that harvesting these types of foods kills the plant completely.

Religious beliefs about what one should and should not eat are so important that in some instances they even influence laws. For example, Hindu lawmakers in many parts of India have passed laws forbidding the slaughter of cows. As a result, in these areas even those young people who belong to other religions are forced into a beef-free diet. Another recent example in which the diets of young people were affected by religious beliefs occurred in 2015. That year there was a proposal to add eggs to school lunches in the state of Madhya Pradesh to reduce the prevalence of underweight and malnourished children there. Advocates of the proposal argued that eggs would be a good source of protein and other nutrients for the children. However, Shivraj Singh Chouhan, the top elected official in the state and a conservative Hindu, rejected the idea, insisting, "The human body is meant to consume vegetarian food, which has everything the human body requires."[82]

Tolerance and Religious Conflict

India is a nation that comprises many different religions, and young people quickly learn the importance of tolerance, since tolerance allows these religions to coexist in Indian society. For hundreds of years, Indians of multiple faiths have managed to live together in relative peace. Indian musician Zakir Hussain says that as he was growing up, his community was so tolerant that he was able to sample various religions without critique. He explains:

My parents were staunch followers of Islam. At home, after my morning prayers and riyaaz [music practice], i would go to a madrasa [Muslim school] and pray. From there, i'd go to St Michael's [Catholic] school, before which i would go to the chapel and say my hymns and novenas. In the evening, i used to go to a [Jewish] temple and then come home to learn tabla [Indian bongo drums] again. No priest or mullah prevented me from doing what i did—i was welcomed into every house of God and i felt blessed in each place.[83]

Although India's many religious groups generally manage to coexist in relative peace, disagreements do occur. These sometimes turn violent and lead to devastating effects on entire communities. Tensions are common between the country's Hindus and Muslims, the two largest religious groups. In 2013, for example, in the Muzaffarnagar District in the northern state of Uttar Pradesh, Hindus attacked Muslim families over claims that Muslim boys had tried to entice Hindu girls. Thousands of Muslim families fled because they feared for their lives, and a large number of them ended up in refugee camps, where many remain. Human rights worker Harsh Mander reported on the status of the displacement three years later, saying, "With mounting astonishment and anguish, we discovered as many as 65 refugee colonies, 28 in Muzaffarnagar and 37 in Shamli, housing 29,328 residents."[84]

As the Muzaffarnagar conflict illustrates, religious loyalties can be fierce in India. However, while divisions such as this do occur, most people in India manage to remain loyal to their religion without antagonizing others, and religion is usually a positive influence on life.

Chapter One: India and Its People

1. Jane Dyson, "Life in the Remote Himalayas Staggers Toward Change," ABC, January 29, 2017. www.abc.net.au.

2. Dyson, "Life in the Remote Himalayas Staggers Toward Change."

3. International Development Exchange, "Partners: India." www.idex.org.

4. Tom Di Liberto, "India Heat Wave Kills Thousands," National Oceanic and Atmospheric Administration, June 9, 2015. www.climate.gov.

5. Quoted in Crystal Chung, "Up on a Roof: Family Sleep Outdoors During Sweltering Indian Summer Heat," Barcroft. www.barcroft.tv.

6. Amrit Dhillon, "Rajasthan, India: Monsoon Magic," *Telegraph* (London), July 26, 2009. www.telegraph.co.uk.

7. Quoted in Steve Richards, "Children Speak About Monsoons and High Hopes in India," World Vision, July 27, 2012. www.worldvision.org.uk.

8. Quoted in Richards, "Children Speak About Monsoons and High Hopes in India."

9. Ritika Katyal, "India Census Exposes Extent of Poverty," CNN, August 2, 2015. www.cnn.com.

10. Kritika Sharma, "The Menace of Underage Driving," *Hindu* (Chennai, India), May 23, 2014. www.thehindu.com.

11. Aastha Sharma, "Why India's Roads Are So Dangerous," *Huffington Post*, July 15, 2016. www.huffingtonpost.in.

12. Quoted in Neal Razzell, "Can India Really Halve Its Road Deaths?," BBC, September 15, 2016. www.bbc.com.

13. Quoted in *Hindustan Times* (New Delhi), "Meet the Young Leaders Hoping to Infuse Vitality into Our Democracy," June 23, 2015. www.hindustantimes.com.

14. Quoted in Joanne O'Connor, "'Every Month for the Next Several Years, 1 Million Indians Will Turn 18,'" *Guardian* (Manchester), April 24, 2016. www.theguardian.com.

15. Quoted in O'Connor, "'Every Month for the Next Several Years, 1 Million Indians Will Turn 18.'"

Chapter Two: Home and Family

16. N.K. Chadha, "Intergenerational Relationships: An Indian Perspective," United Nations. www.un.org.

17. Tanaya Singh, "Life Before and After Electricity—the Tale of 8 Indian Villages," *Better India*, May 5, 2016. www.thebetterindia.com.

18. Nishad Shah, comment on Quora, "What Does It Feel Like to Live in Rural India?," June 14, 2013. www.quora.com.

19. Sandip Pawar, comment on Quora, "Is Life in a Village or in a Small Town Better than City Life?," August 21, 2015. www.quora.com.

20. Saritha Rai, "At Bangalore's Gated Enclaves, the Chaos Outside Comes Knocking at the Door," *India Ink* (blog), *New York Times*, October 29, 2012. https://india.blogs.nytimes.com.

21. Jim Yardley, "In One Slum, Misery, Work, Politics and Hope," *New York Times*, December 28, 2011. www.nytimes.com.

22. Mari Marcel Thekaekara, "Life in an Indian Slum," *New Internationalist* blog, May 6, 2016. https://newint.org.

23. gnocchi649barrage, "Coping with an Entire Culture of Narcissism (India)," Reddit, 2016. www.reddit.com.

24. Stanley Wolpert, *India*. Berkeley: University of California Press, 2005, p. 84.

25. Shreyas Banthalpad, comment on Quora, "What Should Be Preferable, Live in a Joint Family or a Nuclear Family? Why?," April 13 2014. www.quora.com.

26. Apurva Gayakwad, comment on Quora, "How Do Married Couples in India Living with Parents or Joint Families Get Time for Intimacy?," October 14, 2015. www.quora.com.

27. gnocchi649barrage, "Coping with an Entire Culture of Narcissism (India)."

28. Brenda Bhaskar, comment on Quora, "What Is the Difference Between Indian Teens and American Teens?," August 16, 2016. www.quora.com.

29. Dipti Vaid Dedhia, Sheena Vaid Dedhia, and Nina Vaid Raoji, "Here's Why It's Not Weird for Indian Men to Live at Home with Mom and Dad," *Huffington Post*, November 7, 2014. www.huffingtonpost.com.

30. Kavya Sukumar, "Dowries Are Illegal in India. But Families—Including Mine—Still Expect Them," Vox, February 6, 2017. www.vox.com.

31. Utpal M. Dholakia, "Why Are So Many Indian Arranged Marriages Successful?," *The Science Behind Behavior* (blog), *Psychology Today*, November 24, 2015. www.psychology today.com.

32. Upasana Chauhan, "Why I Risked an Honor Killing to Reject an Arranged Marriage," *Time*, August 17, 2016. http://time.com.

33. Balaji Viswanathan, comment on Quora, "Do Arranged Marriages in India Really Work?," July 11, 2014. www.quora.com.

34. Meenakshhi Mishra, comment on Quora, "In India, If Parents Say, 'You May Not Marry This Person,' How Common Is It to Obey (or Conversely, Disobey)?," November 9, 2013. www.quora.com.

35. Sukumar, "Dowries Are Illegal in India. But Families—Including Mine—Still Expect Them."

36. Quoted in Amrit Dhillon, "Worth Their Weight in Humanity," *Age* (Melbourne, Australia), September 30, 2014. www.theage.com.au.

37. Quoted in Jason Koutsoukis, "India Burning Brides and Ancient Practice Is on the Rise," *Sydney Morning Herald*, January 31, 2015. www.smh.com.au.

Chapter Three: Education and Work

38. Brenda Bhaskar, comment on Quora, "What Is the Difference Between Indian Teens and American Teens?," August 16, 2016. www.quora.com.

39. Quoted in *The World*, "In India, Students Can Study Whatever They Want, So Long as Its Engineering," PRI, May 28, 2013. www.pri.org.

40. Quoted in Jillian, "A Kid's Life: India," *Jillian in Italy* (blog), November 22, 2013. https://jillianinitaly.com.

41. Quoted in Nilanjana Bhowmick, "More Children Are Going to School in India, but They're Learning Less," *Time*, July 8, 2014. http://time.com.
42. Quoted in Ann Schraufnagel "India's Need for School Toilets," Pulitzer Center on Crisis Reporting, February 15, 2016. http://pulitzercenter.org.
43. Shourjomoy Ghosh, comment on Quora, "Why There Are Separate Boys and Girls Schools and Colleges in India?," March 17, 2016. www.quora.com.
44. Vijay Prasad, comment on Quora, "Life: What Does It Feel Like to Fail 12th Board Exams?," October 25, 2015. www.quora.com.
45. Jorawar Singh, comment on Quora, "Life: What Does It Feel Like to Fail 12th Board Exams?," March 21, 2016. www.quora.com.
46. Quoted in Craig Jeffrey, "The Students Who Feel They Have the Right to Cheat," BBC, November 9, 2014. www.bbc.com.
47. Quoted in Jeffrey, "The Students Who Feel They Have the Right to Cheat."
48. Quoted in Nazar Abbas, "19,000 Graduates, Postgraduates, MBAs, BTechs Apply for 114 Sweepers' Jobs in UP Town," *Times of India* (Mumbai), January 21, 2016. http://timesofindia.indiatimes.com.
49. Ministry of Human Resource Development, "Some Inputs for Draft National Education Policy," 2016. http://mhrd.gov.in.
50. Quoted in Sabine Dolan, "Former Child Labourers from India Share Their Stories with UNICEF," UNICEF, May 2, 2006. www.unicef.org.
51. Quoted in Dolan, "Former Child Labourers from India Share Their Stories with UNICEF."
52. Mission India, "Bihar: India's Most Illiterate State," February 18, 2015. https://missionindia.org.
53. Ministry of Human Resource Development, "Some Inputs for Draft National Education Policy."

Chapter Four: Social Life

54. Lalit Singh Rajput, comment on Quora, "What Is So Special About Male Friendship in India?," June 5, 2016. www.quora.com.

55. Shreehari K U, comment on Quora, "Why a Guy and a Girl Can Never Be Close Friends in an Indian Society?," August 26, 2016. www.quora.com.

56. Nita J. Kulkarni, "Teenage Sex on the Sly," *A Wide Angle View of India* (blog), September 7, 2006. https://nitawriter.word press.com.

57. Quoted in Nandita Dutta, "Let's Talk About Dating," Little India, August 20, 2012. www.littleindia.com.

58. Quoted in Debarati S. Sen, "Teens Getting Sexually Active Than Ever," *Times of India* (Mumbai), April 16, 2012. http://timesofindia.indiatimes.com.

59. Quoted in Jyoti Sharma Bawa, "Broad-Minded or Bored?," *Hindustan Times* (New Delhi), August 11, 2014. www.mars pvt.net.

60. Ashish Gupta, comment on Quora, "Why Do I See a Lot of Indian Men Holding Hands?," June 4, 2012. www.quora.com.

61. Rajput, comment on Quora, "What Is So Special About Male Friendship in India?"

62. Subash Jayaraman, "Taking It to the Streets," *Cricket Monthly*, May 2015. www.thecricketmonthly.com.

63. Quoted in Rupam Jain, "Kabbadi Is Not an Easy Sport, Says Indian Skipper Tejaswini," *Times of India* (Mumbai), October 8, 2014. http://timesofindia.indiatimes.com.

64. Quoted in Rajini Vaidyanathan, "Chess in India: Why Is It on the Rise?," BBC, May 18, 2012. www.bbc.com.

65. Quoted in Vaidyanathan, "Chess in India."

66. Partho Dasgupta, "Why Television Matters," *Live Mint*, August 20, 2016. www.livemint.com.

67. Julie, "A Tour of the Dharavi Slum in Mumbai, India," *Earth Trekkers* (blog), October 31, 2014. www.earthtrekkers.com.

68. Kavya Guddehithulu Nagesh, comment on Quora, "What Does It Feel Like to Live in Rural India?," April 4, 2013. www .quora.com.

69. Aditya Chakrabortty, "Hanging Out with India's First Real Teenagers," *Guardian* (Manchester), March 29, 2011. www .theguardian.com.

70. Fortis Healthcare, "Impact of Media on Students and Youth," press release, June 21, 2016. http://cdn.fortishealthcare .com.

Chapter Five: Religion

71. Wolpert, *India*, p. 74.
72. Baby Center India, "*Mundan* Ceremony," April 2014. www .babycenter.in.
73. Chhavi Sachdev, "Holy Holi: Colored Powder Will Be Thrown but Splashing Might Be Illegal," NPR, March 23, 2016. www .npr.org.
74. Quoted in Sandeep Rai, "'This Generation Will Be the Last to Skin Cows in India,'" *Times of India* (Mumbai), August 14, 2016. http://timesofindia.indiatimes.com.
75. Chauhan, "Why I Risked an Honor Killing to Reject an Arranged Marriage."
76. Sukhadeo Thorat and Nidhi Sadana Sabharwal, "'Untouchable' in the Classroom," *Toronto Globe and Mail*, September 6, 2012. www.theglobeandmail.com.
77. Wolpert, *India*, pp. 83–84.
78. Wolpert, *India*, p. 84.
79. Quoted in Satya Prakash, "SC Hearing on Gay Sex: All You Need to Know About Section 377," *Hindustan Times* (New Delhi), February 2, 2016. www.hindustantimes.com.
80. Anonymous, comment on Quora, "How Does It Feel to Be Homosexual in India?," August 6, 2015. www.quora.com.
81. Rajesh Sampath, "India Has Outlawed Homosexuality. But It's Better to Be Transgender There than in the U.S.," *Washington Post*, January 29, 2015. www.washingtonpost.com.
82. Quoted in CBS News, "Starving Indian Kids Denied Free Eggs over Religion," July 9, 2015. www.cbsnews.com.
83. Quoted in Sugandha Indulkar, "India Is Tolerant, I'm Proud to Be Indian—and I'm Still Music's Original Heart-Throb: Zakir Hussain," *The Interviews Blog*, *Times of India* (Mumbai), January 25, 2016. http://blogs.timesofindia.indiatimes.com.
84. Harsh Mander, "Muzaffarnagar, Three Years Later," *Indian Express* (Mumbai), September 7, 2016. http://indianexpress .com.

FOR FURTHER RESEARCH

Books

Nishant Anand, *Women in India: The Problem of Missing Girl Child*. New Delhi: New Century, 2016.

Deepita Chakravarty, *Women, Labour and the Economy in India: From Migrant Menservants to Uprooted Girl Children Maids*. New York: Routledge, 2016.

Surinder S. Jodhka, *Caste in Contemporary India*. New Delhi: Routledge, Taylor & Francis Group, 2015.

David Sancho, *Youth, Class and Education in Urban India: The Year That Can Break or Make You*. London and New York: Routledge, 2016.

Vidhu Verma, *Unequal Worlds: Discrimination and Social Inequality in Modern India*. New Delhi: Oxford University Press India, 2015.

Internet Sources

Utpal M. Dholakia, "Why Are So Many Indian Arranged Marriages Successful?," *The Science Behind Behavior* (blog), *Psychology Today*, November 24, 2015. www.psychologytoday.com/blog/the-science-behind-behavior/201511/why-are-so-many-indian-arranged-marriages-successful.

Craig Jeffrey, "The Students Who Feel They Have the Right to Cheat," BBC, November 9, 2014. www.bbc.com/news/magazine-29950843.

Ritika Katyal, "India Census Exposes Extent of Poverty," CNN, August 2, 2015. www.cnn.com/2015/08/02/asia/india-poor-census-secc.

Julie McCarthy, "A Journey of Pain and Beauty: On Becoming Transgender in India," NPR, April 18, 2014. www.npr.org/sections

/parallels/2014/04/18/304548675/a-journey-of-pain-and-beau
ty-on-becoming-transgender-in-india.

Ministry of Human Resource Development, "Some Inputs for Draft National Education Policy," 2016. http://mhrd.gov.in/sites /upload_files/mhrd/files/nep/Inputs_Draft_NEP_2016.pdf.

Varsha Ramakrishnan, "A Broken Promise: Dowry Violence in India," *Johns Hopkins Public Health*, Fall 2013. http://magazine .jhsph.edu/2013/fall/features/a-broken-promise.

Debarati S. Sen, "Teens Getting Sexually Active than Ever," *Times of India*, April 16, 2012. http://timesofindia.indiatimes.com/life -style/relationships/love-sex/Teens-getting-sexually-active-than -ever/articleshow/6119246.cms.

Aastha Sharma, "Why India's Roads Are So Dangerous," *Huffington Post*, July 15, 2016. www.huffingtonpost.in/aastha-sharma -/why-indias-roads-are-so-dangerous.

Tanaya Singh, "Life Before and After Electricity—the Tale of 8 Indian Villages," *Better India*, May 5, 2016. www.thebetterindia .com/54519/job-creation-mnnrega-up.

Mari Marcel Thekaekara, "Life in an Indian Slum," *New Internationalist* blog, May 6, 2016. https://newint.org/blog/2016/05/06 /life-in-an-indian-slum.

United Nations Population Fund, "Dependent, Deprived: Child Brides in India Tell Their Stories," June 10, 2015. www.unfpa.org /news/dependent-deprived-child-brides-india-tell-their-stories.

INDEX

Note: Boldface page numbers indicate illustrations.

Anand, Viswanathan, 50
arranged marriages, 28–30

Bai, Bina, 27
Bai, Tejaswini, 50
Banjara, Puran, 40
Banthalpad, Shreyas, 26
Bemni, 8–9
Bhaskar, Brenda, 27, 34
board exams, 33–34, 36–38
board games, 50
Bollywood, 51
Boulton, Matthew, 18
Brahmins, 57

call center jobs, 37
caste system, 57–60, **60,** 61
cell phones, **53**
    increase in number of, 53–54
    texting by middle-class youth, 51
    using while driving, 17
Centre for the Study of Developing
    Societies, 18
Chadha, N.K., 20
Chadha, Raghav, 18–19
Chakrabortty, Aditya, 51, 54
Chauhan, Upasana, 29, 59
chess, 50
child labor, 40, **41**
child marriage, 27
Chouhan, Shivraj Singh, 65
Christianity, percentage of population, 7
CIA World Factbook
    child labor, 40
    Indo-Aryans and Dravidians as
        percentage of population, 13
    percentage of population living below
        poverty line, 14
climate, 10–12, **12**
CNN, 13–14

collectivist culture, 15
cows, 64, 65
cricket, 48–49, **49**

Dalits, 57–60, **60,** 61
Dasgupta, Partho, 52
dating, 44–45
Deccan Plateau, **6,** 10
Dedhia, Dipti, 27–28
Dedhia, Sheena Vaid, 27–28
Dhillon, Amrit, 11
Dholakia, Utpal M., 28
discrimination by caste, 58–60, **60**
Dravidians, percentage of population, 13
Dyson, Jane, 8–9

education
    absenteeism among teachers, 42
    career choices and, 34
    college standards, 39
    discrimination against Dalit children,
        59–60
    exams, 33–34, 36–38
    funding variations, 34–35
    gender and, 9, 25, 35–36
    Hindu religious texts in, 58
    jobs for college graduates, 37, 38–40,
        39
    lack of electricity and, 21
    literacy, 7, 41–42
    pressure to succeed, 25, 33
    required, 33
electricity, 20–21, 24
End of Karma, The (Sengupta), 19
engineering, as career choice, 34
ethnic groups, 7, 13
"Eve teasing," 47

family
    extended, in one house, 25–26
    importance of, 15, 20
    parent-child relationship
        career choices, 34

care for elderly parents, 27–28
marriage and, 27, 28–30, 44
parental control over everyday life,
    26–27, 44–45
responsibilities of women and girls, 9,
    20, **21**, 25
Fernandes, Donna, 31
Festival of Color, 56, **57**
flag, **6**
food and religion, 64–65
Fortis Healthcare study, 54

Ganges River, **6**, 9–10, **10**
Gayakwad, Apurva, 26
gender
    arranged marriages and, 29
    creation of recognition of third, 62–63
    dowries, 30–32
    education and, 9, 25, 35–36
    family responsibilities and, 25
        care of elderly parents, 28
        water collection, 9, 20, **21**
    friendships and, 44–45, **46**, 47–48
    sports and, 50
geography, 8–10
Ghosh, Shourjomoy, 35–36
government, 7, 17–19
Gupta, Ashish, 47–48

health, vaccination, 18
Himalayas (Himalaya Mountains), **6**, 8–9
Hindi, 13
Hindu (newspaper), 15–16
Hinduism
    caste system, 57–60, **60,** 61
    holidays, 56, **57**
    homosexuality and, 61–62, **63**
    life cycle rituals, 55–56
    percentage of population, 7, 55
    reincarnation belief, 61
    tensions and violence with Muslims,
        66
    transgender people and, 62–63, **63**
    use of religious texts in public schools,
        58
Hingorrany, Seema, 45–46
Holi, 56, **57**
homes
    extended family living together, 25–26
    in rural areas, 20

in Thar Desert, 9
in urban areas, 22–25, **24**
homosexuality, 61–62, **63**
HT-MaRS Youth Survey, 46
Huffington Post (newspaper), 36
Hussain, Zakir, 65

illiteracy, 7, 41–42
India, basic facts about, **6,** 7
India's Socioeconomic and Caste
    Census, 13–14
Indo-Aryan percentage of population,
    13
Indo-Gangetic Plain, 9–10
industries, 7, 51
International Development Exchange, 9
*International Journal of Applied
    Research*, 15
Internet
    marriage matchmaking websites,
        28–29
    number of users, 7
    "text-speak," 51
Islam, 55
    food prohibition, 64
    Jama Masjid (mosque), **53**
    percentage of population, 7
    tensions and violence with Hindus, 66

Jainism, 64–65
Jan, Shafeer, 31
Jayaraman, Subash, 48–49
Jeffrey, Craig, 37
jobs
    call center, 37
    child labor, 40, **41**
    lack of, for college graduates, 37,
        38–40, **39**
    teachers, 42
Joshi, Aneesh, 15

kabaddi, 49–50
Kohli, Ambika, 47
Kolkata, **6, 12**
Kshatriyas, 57
Kulkarni, Nita J., 45
Kumari, Golu, 35

languages, 7, 13
literacy, 7, 41–42

Mahabharata, 58, 63
Maharajsaheb, Acharya Vimalsagarsuriji, 64
Mander, Harsh, 66
marriage, **29**
    caste system and, 59
    child, 27
    dowries, 30–32
    parental control and, 28–30, 44
medicine, as career choice, 34
Mishra, Manoj, 42
Mishra, Meenakshhi, 30
Mission Indradhanush, 18
Mohamad, Samsur, 40
monsoon season, 11–12, **12**
movies, 51
Mumbai, **6**
    film industry, 51
    ninth graders driving in, 15
    traffic accidents in, 17
Mund, Yasmin, 11
Murgai, Avneesh, 46

Nagesh, Kavya Guddehithulu, 52–53
name, official, 7
Nath, Abhijnan, 37
National Oceanic and Atmospheric Administration, 10
New Dehli, **6**
    climate, 10–11
    Holi in, 56
    location, **6,** 10
New York Times (newspaper), 29, 42

Pal, Ovindra, 58–59
Patel, Rima, 45
Pawar, Sandip, 22
People's Linguistic Survey of India, 13
Phalisiya, Murtaza, 34
Poojari, Mamta, 50
population, 7
    compared to China, 12–13
    Dravidians as percentage of, 13
    ethnic diversity, 7, 13
    Indo-Aryans as percentage of, 13
    on Indo-Gangetic Plain, 10
    number of third-gender people, 62
    percentage living below poverty line, 14
    youth, 7, 8, 13, 19

poverty
    child labor, 40, **41**
    city slums, 23–24, **24**
    percentage living below poverty line, 14
    public bathing, 23
    rural, 13–14
Prasad, Vijay, 36
premarital sex, 45–47
privacy, lack of, 23, 25, 26

Rai, Saritha, 22–23
Rajput, Lalit Singh, 44, 48
Rajvanshi, Anil K., 58
Ramraje, Dhananjay, 50
Raoji, Nina Vaid, 27–28
reincarnation, 61
religion, 7
    food and, 64–65
    importance of, in everyday life, 55, 61
    Jainism, 64–65
    major, originating in India, 55
    Sikhism, 7
    tolerance for different, 65–66
    See also Hinduism; Islam
Richards, Steve, 12
roads, 14–17
rural areas
    absence of electricity, 20–21
    child labor, 40, **41**
    child marriage, 27
    education, 42
    in Himalayas, 8–9
    homes, 20
    households with television, 52
    percentage of population living in, 13
    poverty, 13–14
    social life, 21–22
    water collection, 20, 21, **21**

Sabharwal, Nidhi Sadana, 59–60
Sachdev, Chhavi, 56
Sampath, Rajesh, 62–63
sanitation
    access to clean water and toilets, 14, **24**
    in poor schools, 35
    in slums, **24,** 24–25
Sengupta, Somini, 19
sexual harassment, 47

77

Shah, Nishad, 22
Sharma, Aastha, 17
Sharma, Kritika, 15–16
Shudras, 57
Sikhism, 7
Singh, Jorawar, 36–37
Singh, Nakul, 38–39
Singh, Pinki, 38
Singh, Pratap, 37
Singh, Tanaya, 21
social life
  board games, 50
  dating and premarital sex, 45–47
  extended family and, 26
  friendships and gender, 44–45, **46,**
    47–48
  hanging out in urban areas, 51
  movies, 51
  in rural areas, 21–22
  sexual harassment, 47
  social media, 51, **53,** 53–54
  sports, 48–50, **49**
  television, 52–53
sports, 48–50, **49**
Stephen, Becky, 15, 23
Sukumar, Kavya, 28, 31
Sukumar, Srini, 28

Tekukar, Aadva, 50
Tekukar, Shubangi, 50
television, 52–53
"text-speak," 51
Thar Desert, **6,** 9
Thekaekara, Mari Marcel, 25
Thorat, Sukhadeo, 59–60
Times of India (newspaper)
  census including third gender, 62
  lack of jobs for college graduates, 38
  lack of sewage treatment, 14
  ninth graders driving, 15
transgender people, 62–63, **63**
Transparency International, 42
transportation, 14–17, **16**

U, Shreehari K, 44–45
United Nations Population Fund, 8, 27
University of Michigan School of Public
  Health, 18
untouchables, the (Dalits), 57–60, **60,** 61
urban areas
  gated communities, 22–23
  hanging out at malls, 51
  households with television, 52
  increase in population, 14
  lack of sanitation services, 14
  marriage in, 30
  premarital sex in, 46–47
  slums, 23–25, **24**

vaccines, 18
vegetarianism, 64–65
Viswanathan, Balaji, 30
"Volatile" stage, 44

water
  collection in rural areas, 9, 20, **21**
  contamination, 14
  public bathing and, 23
  in slums, 24–25
WaterAid, 14
We Are Social, 53
Wolpert, Stanley
  on effect of belief in reincarnation, 61
  on extended family, 25–26
  on importance of religion in everyday
    life, 55

Yardley, Jim, 24
youth
  child marriage, 27
  driving by, 14–16, **16**
  illiterate, 41–42
  interest in politics, 18–19
  opinion of accuracy of information on
    social media, 54
  population, 7, 8, 13, 19
  vaccination of children, 18

PICTURE CREDITS

Cover: Thinkstock Images/Jaimaa85

6: Maury Aaseng

7: Shutterstock.com

10: Shutterstock.com/Zvonimir Altetic

12: Associated Press

16: Shutterstock.com/Radiokafka

21: Associated Press

24: Shutterstock.com/Narit Jindajamorn

29: Shutterstock.com/Bodom

35: Hindustan Times/Newscom

39: Associated Press

41: Associated Press

46: Sebastian Kahnert/Picture Alliance/dpa-Zentralbi/Newscom

49: Shutterstock.com/Tukaram Karve

53: Sauvik Acharyya/Zuma Press/Newscom

57: Vikramjit Kakati/Zuma Press/Newscom

60: Divyakant Solanki/EPA/Newscom

63: © Avalon

Andrea C. Nakaya, a native of New Zealand, holds a BA in English and an MA in communications from San Diego State University. She has written and edited more than forty books on current issues. She currently lives in Encinitas, California, with her husband and their two children, Natalie and Shane.